Florent-Alain BIKINI MUSINI

I0439533

Africa is Bleeding:
Between Miseries and Hopes

Preface of Jean-Paul Eschlimann

SMA Publications
www.smainternational.info

Translated from French into English by Gbortsu Fabian, PhD in Religious Studies specializing on African Traditional Morality, from the Catholic University of Eastern Africa (CUEA), Nairobi, Kenya.

ISBN-13: 978-1533117199
ISBN-10: 1533117195

© SMA Publications, Rome, avril 2016.

To those who have ended their lives in the desert of Sahara and at the bottom of the Mediterranean sea, the Atlantic ocean in open and silent graves in search of new beginnings in the European Eldorado.

To my dad Isidore BIKINI MUDIANDAMBU and my bother Papy BIKINI MOKE who are now resting in peace.

To my mother Rosalie MUNDONI DEDE who continues to struggle for the BIKINI family.

To Jean-Paul ESCHLIMANN, Josette KIENTZLER, André N'KOY and Fabian Gbortsu for their support.

Books published in the same collection, *Mission, Spirituality and Testimonials*

BONFILS Jean (Mgr), *Disciples pour la Mission*, 178 pages.

BURROWS D. Peter, *On the Reading of Scripture: Elijah, the Prophet*, 2015, 132 pages.

CULLINANE Tim, *Journeying to SMA priesthood*, 2014, 188 pages.

ESCHLIMANN Jean-Paul & TRICHET Pierre, *Monuments funeraires en Cote d'Ivoire*, 2016, 86 pages.

THEBAULT Jean, *Va… là où je t'enverrai (Jérémie 1,7)*, 2014, 172 pages.

THEBAULT Jean, *Ils veulent vivre dans la dignité*, 2015, 152 pages.

TRICHET Pierre, *Sir James Marshall : Une passion pour une Afrique chrétienne*, 2014, 136 pages.

ROESCH Charles, *Souvenirs de mission au Togo (1956-2006)*, 2015, 236 pages.

Preface

From time to time, the media move the European public opinion on the dramatic situation of African immigrants, who try to cross over to the Maltese, Italian and Spanish coasts but whose boats usually capsize at sea. A recent chronicle which appeared in the La Croix Newspaper written by Bruno Frappat, spoke of the Mediterranean Sea as a "marine cemetery". He wrote among others things:

> *This week (...), five hundred clandestine immigrants have perished between Malta and Sicily. It appeared that they sunk because the smugglers have decided to do away with them for whatever reason the justice system will find difficult to explain. The day where a news dispatch of the AFP (Agence France Presse) broke the story of the dangerous/deadly shipwreck, there was no mention of it during the prime time news on France 2. Not a single tear was shed for the Somalians, Malians, Ethiopians, Palestinians of the Gaza strip and Syrians who have all paid a fortune (more than 1 000€, per person-without doubt) in order to reach Europe, whose prospects are wondrous in their sight, its societies that they imagined are welcoming, were in the ignorance of the fact that Europe has stiffen its hostility to immigration (...). The young, the elderly and families they board the ships with their poor "barda" and their illusory treasures, thinking that we shall welcome them with open arms. They could not imagined that they will be ending only at the bottom of the sea in a silent grave and that their "last resting place", all illusions swallowed, will be a bed of darkness of hell*.

All these, like the case of the previous dramas, had passed in total indifference of the Europeans and the African leaders. Nobody protested against the cynicism of the smugglers and had no compassion for these migrants looking for life and better living.

It is precisely in front of these anonymous disappearances, these dead without graves, that Florent-Alain is indignant.

---

1. Cimetière marin, Bruno FRAPPAT, L'humeur des jours, *La croix* du samedi 20 septembre 2014, p.28.

These deaths are for him the symbol of a rejected continent, excluded from history. The author cannot accept that these shipwreck in history be considered a "bad death", that they become those who eternally hunt the world like shadows, according to the expected tradition (of Africa and probably of the countries of origin of the dead). For them therefore, he wants to do the work of "remembrance"; he assures them a place in history and in collective conscience so as to wrestle them from the condemned hands of oblivion.

Then, he is captivated by their drama. This massive exodus/exile of the African youths to the "European Eldorado" is a painful thorn in the flesh. He attempts to elucidate the causes. To this end, for more than ten years he has interviewed many youths in many African countries; he has read and worked on many works speaking about the same problem in many different ways; he approached couples which were successful and now living in Europe to work there and to make their lives there. He himself know the two sides of the situation: his childhood and formation in Kinshasa and then with the African Missions; his studies in the University of Strasbourg complemented by Summer Courses at Yale University in New Haven Connecticut in the United States; finally, his engagement in the Church of Alsace as a pastor of a parish. He occupies a privileged position in order to appreciate the essential dimensions of the problem which preoccupies him, analysing them and to make an original contribution to them.

His position is clear: nobody can excuse himself from the present situation of Africa; neither Africa, nor Europe, not the youth, not the leaders of the various countries. Nobody can run away from his/her responsibilities. In the search for the causes of this "suicidal journey" of some of the youth of Africa, the author emphasise the relevance of the weight of the "past" on present African societies. The traces left behind after four centuries of the Trans-Atlantic slave trade and almost a century of colonisation, make Africa a person-object, of second class, subservient, exploited at the mercy of works that others do not want to undertake. In their own land, the people cannot expect but a life of misery, perpetuating the ancestral discriminatory institutions, especially for women left to the bite of famine, wars, and deadly epidemics. This is an accumulation of suffering on the black skin, which the "outside" is not the only responsible, but which the people of Africa and their leaders maintain without ceasing.

It is altogether relevant to denounce the human, economic and social consequences of the slave trade and the colonisation. It would also be necessary to throw light on how these situations actually moult/evolve and perpetuate itself under our eyes, without even moving African themselves. And so, a multinational like Benetton, buys a whole province in Patagonia to rear the sheep with the highest quality wool necessary for the fabrication of their product, but at the price of appropriating the land and dispossessing of the local people, reducing them to only the agricultural work force without pay or as simple recluses without land! And so China buys whole mineral regions in Africa, monopolises trade, de-structuralise the local informal economy, without employing a single local worker or concerns herself with the wellbeing of the people. The Chinese leaders bring in their own workers, their businesses etc., to the detriment of local needs.

This present book also overlooks what seems as essential to the malaise in Africa: the dual and symbiotic relationships between the former colonies and the West. Because of their singular history, the people of Africa are caught in a "stunning" relationship almost completely linking them to Europe, the land of the former colonial masters. It should be possible to break this total hold on the relationship and of fascination, which establishes a sort slave master relationship, and open it to others. This other can be Asia, through the developing countries which are found there. The history of the slave trade and of colonisation will not hijack this relationship and would serve as a mediation of the African conscience to renegotiate her relationships with her past and the West. And so, why are young African choosing migration and not taking the Asian route?

In the ocean of misery described in the first part of the book, Florent-Alain Bikini foresees some islands of hope, to which he consecrated the second part of the book. With true reasons, he indicated in the first place education of the people especially the youth. He was passionate about the role that the Enlightenment played in Europe and invite Africa also to criticise her own "reason". The way forward is interesting. But it seems that he has not thrown enough light on what this "cultural revolution" will mean as transformation on the transmission of the traditional cultures, greatly influence by silence, the secret, religious control, social status, sex and power.

A question arises: is education all about access to knowledge and modern technologies and their accumulation? Will technological expertise, all of sudden, erase misery in Africa? I remember a good and a lived example. Benoît (Benedict), a good friend from Cote d'Ivoire, a civil engineer who graduated from the prestigious *Ecole Nationale d'Agronomie* (The French Institute of/School of Agronomy) of Paris, was not able to improve, even in the least, the traditional farming practices of his parents when he returned to Cote d'Ivoire. His parents continued going to the farm on foot, bring back food stuff from the farm on the head, using the same farm implements (cutlass and hoe) to work the field, hunting to get some meat for eating, etc. Benedict was not able to use the resources and the know-how of his family, to even create a small system of irrigation in his region of origin which would have needed of it or to introduce farming or transportation by harness, etc. This raises big questions: is it enough to obtain certificates in western universities, master knowledge and have technical expertise, to think that education is successful and that it will modify the conditions life in Africa? How can we adapt the qualifications and competencies obtained to the specific African mentality? How to transmit these competencies in such a way as to arouse creativity in the people of African? The present work has not raised these questions. They will certainly be raised in a later work.

In the process of education, the author examines the issue of development. He advocates for the deconstruction of present discourses which obeys the vision of things coming from outside. The structural adjustments, imposed by the IMF on African countries, are the paradigmatic examples. We know the devastating effects on the people and the local economies. Instead of reducing poverty and misery, they have aggravated them. The author is fighting for a development which gives the possibility of talking to the beneficiaries themselves and puts the definition of the objectives as well as the execution in their hands.

The big hope of change in the eyes of Florent-Alain Bikini, resides in the promotion of equality and empowerment of women. Victims of the sexual division of labour (gender division of labour), of the patriarchal chauvinistic relationships, of the impossibility to have access to land, of a marriage system characterised by the payment of excessive dowry which makes of the woman a "property" of a man who had to have her, women are excluded from progress and development. They nonetheless represent the base of the informal economy. If they were liberated from the cultural constraints, from their dependence on men, if they could benefit from the access of education on a massive scale, they would have become a productive force and a source of progress in the Africa of tomorrow.

Africa is bleeding! But it is rather the heart of Florent-Alain Bikini which is bleeding. The page which describes his passage at the "La Porte du non Retour"/"Gate of No Return" in Ouidah (Benin), through which the slave left for the new world without any hope of coming back to their native land is moving. He did not hesitate to write in the first person, to assume the history, to announce his choices and to propose his perspectives for the future. He thus forbids us to treat casually the problem of clandestine immigration between Africa and Europe, to reduce them to cyclical episodes, which will finish by disappearing from the collective memory! He demonstrates the futility of European policy of control and limitation of immigration, in showing that there is a powerful human history and an unquenchable desire for wellbeing that push people to migrate risking their life in the desert and on the Mediterranean Sea.

It is urgent that young Africans and their leaders, as well as political leaders in Europe, listen profoundly to the invitation of this book. I am grateful to the author to have raised his voice that this human drama does not become a thing forgotten of history or is not reduced to a minor incident in world history, which continues to grind Africa and to treat her as a negligible entity. I also recognise his merit of wanting to awaken the African conscience so as to take her destiny in her own hand and to confront her situation head on. Those involved should find the courage and the necessary human resources to create a cultural, economic and religious environment which promotes healing from malaise of the societies of the continent.

In his conclusion, the author evokes a "dream" which particularly interested me, to which I would like to be a founding reality. He wrote especially: "Our dream is to see in a near future in Africa ..., a general state on the youth sacrificed by clandestine immigration. May the voice of Africa be heard at last, in a way that something else may be proposed to the youth rather than the clandestine immigration towards the European mirage." It seems that such a project can be started by the help of the Church, of both catholic and protestant universities and of religious congregations. They will be an engine to bring in their wake political leaders and the international community, always slow to mobilise.

This is a proverb of the Agni people in Cote d'Ivoire: "If you carry the load to your knees, God will put it on your head". That the youth and the African leaders may hear it!

Jean-Paul ESCHLIMANN

INTRODUCTION

This is a crossed analytical study with a conscious and pragmatic approach of social and historical issues of Africa in order to draw some essential elements for the construction of a common and better destiny (future). Clandestine immigration of young Africans from the sub-Saharan region is the cause of this reflection in order to determine the 'why' of the bad state of black Africa of today. Digging into our past is the challenge we give ourselves in order to establish in equal measure /parts the different responsibilities implied in the disaffection of Africa today: Europe, America and Africa. Through its leaders and youth, no one can claim innocence for what the Africa continent is passing through actually. Our research in the field in countries and among the people with whom we have lived (the two Congo's, Togo, Ghana, Benin, Nigeria, Cote d'Ivoire, Central African Republic, Kenya, Tanzania, and Uganda) constitute an impulse and a strong basis and statistics which permits us to affirm that more than one out of two youths no longer believe in the capacity of our leaders, neither do they believe in the possibility of a better future. In a sample of hundred youths between the ages of 20 and 30 years with both sexes, interrogated on the three following questions:

1. In your opinion, what are the real causes for the sad delay of Africa's situation as regard its development?

2. To live a decent life, which projects are urgently needed to be put in place? and

3. Which challenges must Africa overcome in order to be more attractive to the youth?

The responses and replies are varied according as interrogated girls or boys. It is also varied according to economic and political factors of each of the countries. This research started in the year 2000. It ended in 2013 making duration of 13 years in the field and thus permitting us to refine our thematic approach, to renew first and foremost the methodology and to constitute statistical information which at the time of the final editing seems credible and better refined. Despite regional differences and disparities in the replies a common ground emerged with certitude on some viewpoints that we are obliged to mention in order to establish the plan of this book. We have opted for a difficult task; that of putting together the information, forgetting the distances between the ten countries above in which the research took place, representing the totality that we may call, wrongly perhaps, black Africa.

We have bracketed out minimal differences in the replies and privileged the common points of view in the responses and replies. This detail on the method used is important for the obvious reason of understanding the spirit in which the book was written. This is the gaze of an African who has charged himself with the duty of questioning the traumatic past statistics with the view of drawing lessons in order to construct a radiant future. To the first question of the real causes of the sad situation of Africa, three responses came out strongly: the slave trade, colonisation and the lack of credible political elite. To the second question the urgency seem to be the flight from misery and the search for the Western Eldorado. To the last question, the youth are pleading for good governance, putting infrastructures in place, and the preponderant place and role of education. The proposed responses of the youth constitute the plan of the book to be divided into two main parts: I.) The Miseries, and II.) The Hopes based on the desires and pious wishes of a better day in the future. We shall start with clandestine immigration which seem to us as the biggest expression of disappointment in the Continent by its treasured young force which is the youth.

I. THE MISERIES

Before we start this first part which concern Africa in her totality, we would like to briefly present our country of origin the DRC, the Democratic Republic of Congo. It is a vast country, the second in Africa after Algeria. This big country four time the size of France shares boarders with nine African countries if Angola, Burundi, Central African Republic, Congo Brazzaville, Rwanda, Uganda, South Sudan, Tanzania, and Zambia. In the world, only China, Russia, and Brazil have more than DRC each of the above have ten to fourteen neighbours. David van Reybrouck made this remark of the linguistic and cultural homogeneity of the country:

> *Almost all the languages are Bantu and they present a similar internal structure (Bantu is the plural of Muntu which means 'the people')*[2].

We are pointing out among other things that, this country is agro-pastoral with the land as her endowed economic gift and one of the factors for production. Kinshasa is the capital of DRC and is situated in the western part of the country. We will be coming often on the subject of this nation finding it difficult to take-off economically despite all her potentialities.

I.1. Clandestine immigration

Clandestine immigration is one of the evils of the African youth that destroy and subjugate our continent today. Strangely enough, this subject is not raised or if raised not followed through enough by the very leaders who hold the destiny of the continent in their hand. They do not have the will to see. Political leaders, government officials, pastors and opinion leaders do not seem to grasp the full measure of this cancer which costs the life of many desperate and disoriented African youth who want to try, at all cost everything for everything, in order to survive elsewhere. A Ghanaian youth

---

2. REYBROUCK van David, *Congo, une histoire*, Amsterdam, Actes Sud, 2012, p. 30.

describes his desire to run away from his desperate misery in the following manner:

"The adventure is life or death. The one who does not risk has nothing. Me, I prefer dying to renouncing my leaving, said a Ghanaian. When one flees misery, nothing can stop you. Absolutely nothing. Today, I want to leave. Please say it well: I am afraid of nothing, not the wind, not the rain, not eve bullets. Very soon, I will be in Melilla. We shall see the rest after, he concluded."[3]

Immigration is a personal re-location into the world of others. The reasons for the departure vary from country to country. However, the many wars and the miseries which Africa is going through are the first causes. For a reduction in this flux situation, they must be taken seriously into consideration.

Whatever the cause may be, two representation dominates the thought of those who leave: on the one hand is the protection and social security represented by the welfare state or the Eldorado towards which everyone goes and on the other hand the insecurity and misery which represent the countries of origin. African leaders do not want to look at a history that disturbs, which annoys, which bewilderment, which maybe is to the disadvantage of some. This silence is killing us. The leaders are silent maybe because they have no alternatives to propose to the youth who are our children, our friends, who have become like suicide bombers not of terrorism but like sacrificed lamb who dare the hopelessness of the waves, the storm and the maritime difficulties to endure the humiliating part of exile. The Sahara desert, the Atlantic ocean and the Mediterranean Sea have become today an open grave. The days, the weeks, the months and the years pass and no one counts the numbers of those lost in this tragedy without trace.

---

3. DANIEL Serge, *Les routes clandestines. L'Afrique des immigrés et des passeurs*, Paris, Hachette, 2008, p. 52

Our youth have become blind to the beauty and the formidable future of Africa and so by way of hopelessness prefer to leave for other lands in search of work and money. Leaving is, in the first place, a consequence of an unbearable situation which uproots and separates from loved ones and ones roots. One of the major causes of the African youth's new exile to Europe and the USA, particularly of Congolese men and women, is the search for better conditions of life.

If we can believe Dambisa Moyo, a former consultant for the World Bank who is of zambian origin, that more difficult days are to come for Africa:

> *"And looking ahead, the 2007 United Nations Human Development Report forecasts that sub-Saharan Africa will account for almost one third of the world poverty in 2015, up from one fifth in 1990"*[4].

Many of our countries are late in taking off economically because of lack of good governance and credible institutions as well as the corrupt practices which leave nothing for the poor of the poor but the only option of exile and all forms of contemporary migration. Is there anything more frustrating and anything more chocking than to live without hope of a better future? Why does it seem that the history of African is excluded from that of the whole world? The exclusion of Africa, of her problems, of her history, of her art, of her culture is like a gigantic monster using the expression of Joseph Ki-Zerbo:

> *"Slowly and slowly, this exclusion appears to me as a gigantic monster. I was thirsty while studying the Middle Ages of Europe or the contemporary period, in order to know the history of Africa. It started to interest me because, her absence makes us uneasy and made us thirst, and rightly so. The desire to exhume her history and to own it is born from this contradiction[5]."*

4. DAMBISA Moyo, *Dead Aid. Why aid is not working and how there is a better way for Africa*, New York, Farrar, Straus and Giroux, 2010, p. 5.
5. KI-ZERBO Joseph, *A quand l'Afrique?*, Paris, Editions de l'Aube, 2003, p. 11.

17

Now, I am looking for the reason why Africa is not attractive, or let us say why Africa does not interest others? Just imagine a single instance whereby American or European youth are in search of a better life and left to their own fate in the plague of the desert or the sea and not making the first headlines of all the media of the world? Should one be part of a particular race when in danger? The silence bomb which is clandestine immigration is causing a great havoc in terms of human life of Africa. These dead people interrogate us. To give a fitting reply we must tackle the cause of this tragedy. I have chosen to write in order to honour the memory, to raise it as an issue of debate, to save the last of the boats so as to prevent another boast tragedy and total disappearance of Africa. Why is it that no one or very few people say something openly about this human drama with the victims? The true debate is late in coming into the public domain.

It concerns first of all, if one honest with him or herself, about the equitable sharing of the resources of Africa. On our planet there is a terrible gap and a horrible displacement on the one hand of the exuberances of the rich from Western countries and on the other hand the abject poverty of the third world countries especially that of Africa. Do you know many of the youth have already died or dying now trying to cross the desert and then the Atlantic in the bid to reach the uninhabited arid zones and forests of the Spanish enclave of Melilla and Cueta or the Italian territory of Lampedusa? Are you aware of the kind of inhuman treatment meted out on these people by the Algero-Morocan Interpol? For only the first six months of 2006, on Radio France International (RFI), a Spanish humanitarian organisation SOS Racismo assured having counted about 2,400 (two thousand four hundred) clandestine Africans on buses chartered by the Moroccan authorities. Thereafter, they were transported by force to the edge of the Moroccan desert on the border with Algeria and Mauritania. The humanitarian organisation does not know what happened to two thirds of the clandestine Africans on the fateful bus to the Moroccan desert which boarders Algeria and Mauritania. Since the year 2000 men and women have taken to the desert as one discharges garbage.

In the developed countries facilities to recycle exist, but black Africans abandoned in the desert are not good enough and are left to die of hunger and thirst. Life is hereby thrown to the throes of death. The destiny of these wretched human beings are left hanging and clinging unto the economic and political interest of powerful nations. Presenting his book *"Mamadou va mourir"* meaning *Mamadou will die*, Gabriele del Grande who has close interest in clandestine immigration accused Europe for having close her eyes to human rights violations by handing over boarder controls to Morocco, Algeria and Libya. For more than 20 years now uncountable numbers of young people from Africa simply die of hypothermia, dehydration or getting drowned in the ocean. One decries the human right violations including rapes, deportations, torture and denial of freedom, which will probably never be brought before any court for justice to be seen to have been done. The impunity of the perpetrators at the boarders seems the rule of the game and has become normal. Abbé Pierre, a French catholic priest, who took to heart the cause of the poor and the homeless, invited the whole world to act in order to overcome the rapidly spreading menace. The rich world is only slowly waking up to the extent of the suffering of the poor of our world:

> *To overcome misfortune, let us be courageous to open the eyes and fight. The world is suffering. Those of us who are not hungry, who are neither without work, nor without a home, can we live what the unimaginable difficulties of others ask of us? The word is suffering, probably more than ever[6].*

Yes the world is suffering but Africa beats all the others in suffering, misery, catastrophes, marginalisation, poverty and pauperisation. She

---

6. Abbé Pierre, *Testament*, Paris, Bayard, 1995, p. V.

lacks the opportunity to take off and so reach and propose a decent condition to her children.

That is why the youth choose to leave for the developed world. The desire and the need to live decent life always lead to migration, a phenomenon known to humanity since the dawn of history. In the past, the people of Israel went to Egypt in order to run away from faming and misery in their land. For the same reason, after the so called discovery of America in 1492 by Christopher Colombo, Europeans went to conquer the new world. There in the new world, the English, the Spanish and the Portuguese created colonies for themselves. One remembers that after that, the so-called well known explorers like Henry Morton Stanley, David Livingstone, Pierre Savorgnan de Brazza came to Africa and since then she has been subjected to exploitation and colonisation without mercy. European came to stay in order to take advantage of the human and natural patrimony of Africa. We shall come back to this period of history and that which followed after it.

History is repeating itself only for this time that it is African who are knocking at the doors of others. Tired of suffering at home, they leave their own country. They want to go to other places which are better as it is the case always. The world has always evolved because of these revolts. Let us simply say that no legitimate barrier can stop the poor from going to greener pastures. L'Abbé Pierre, a fervent defender and one in solidarity with the poor and the weak went further in the aforesaid in the following terms:

This time is that of powerlessness of the powerful and an unbelievable power of the weak."[7]

These youth have nothing to lose and so take all chances presented to them in all directions: the Island of Malta, the Canaries, Cueta, Melilla, Lampedusa. In Africa they die all the time of poverty and diseases. They lack public transport, adequate education, work, and

---

7. Abbé Pierre, *Op. Cit.*, p. 35.

so to die drowned in the sea or in the desert is no longer a frightening situation for them. Nothing can stop the victims of the European mirage. Nothing can stop the migration flow from the start. As long as poverty puts the lives of a section of humanity into danger, alternative routes will be taken. In June 2007 at the time while I was writing these lines, images were shown on the television screens of France 24 where one can see small frigate, a French warship was seen recovering bodies in advanced stages of decomposition in the Maltese waters. They were sent to Toulon for identification. In the same waters, on 2nd June 2007 and that was two weeks earlier, one could hear on the same France 24 the cries of distress of clandestine immigrants whose boat was capsized. Some were saved because of tuna fish cages near to the place of their boarding and on which they clung for safety.

There is another issue that we want to be properly recorded, and that is the behaviour of the Congolese diaspora once back to Congo. The Congolese migratory imagery is nourished by both the language and the behaviours of those who come back from their European adventure. To those near them, they give an attractive style of life which makes one to think that life is all luxury. With money kept aside for years during physically tasking and difficult work in the West, they live a style of life far different from what they had before embarking on their adventure. Seeing them it looks like a dream for those who cannot make it at home. With many deceptive trappings they defy the leaders of the country showing to them that without them, they can still make it in life to succeed elsewhere.

This extravagance does not hide their hatred of the corrupted powerful who misuses the resources of the state. We note here also the influence in the two Congo of music with a preponderance place and which does not stop to sing the better quality of Paris and Brussels. Artists on both side of the Congo River have enormously contributed to give a false image to the youth that immigration is the unique solution to make them come out of poverty:

"In their lyrics, the musician artists of both shores of the Congo River do not stop, in the course of the 70s and 80s, to evoke the joy of working and living in Europe... They also sing the 'beautiful life' illustrated by 'Sape' (that is wearing in particular flamboyant Parisian marks and other world marks in general), as well as the issue of working and earning more elsewhere than in Congo (direct exchange rate of the nominal value of salary of country of work and country of origin, the level of income comparable with high government workers if not more, but more than this in reality it is the purchasing power which should be compared), the possibility to give financial help to family left behind in the country, in short the material privileges of life in Europe. The 'sapeur'; in this case the present praise-singers of old, sociologists of the present, tried to express their sentiments and issues of this fringe movement of population of the two Congo."[8]

We see then that the need and the interest to leave Congo are fuelled by many causes. Apart from the insecurity as a result of the war, we can say that the major cause of the Congolese youth leaving their native country of origin.

It is the case in many other countries of Africa, which are the object of this research, even if it is to different degrees. The poor do not want to always stay and die in poverty and misery; they leave in order to risk it elsewhere. The DRC even though is endowed with many mineral resources does not allow a good part of her youth to earn their living in Congo. In the absence of a bright future, pessimism opens the way for optimism elsewhere for a better tomorrow. The war, poverty, in one case as in the other, migration

---

8. DOUMA Jean-Baptiste, *L'immigration Congolaise en France. Entre crises et recherche de l'identité*, Paris, L'Harmattan, 2003, p. 8-9.

of the Congolese youth becomes the practice of security of a life in search for wellbeing.

Everybody must put their hand to it, including the African youth, so as to give the possibility to these clandestine men and women to live and to work in their own country. Not long ago Michel Rocard, the former French Prime Minister said that France cannot welcome all the misery of the world.

It is all together true that no country will commit such a fatal error. It is also true that France and all other slave driven countries and colonial countries cannot in no way run away from the initial momentum they sent in motion regarding this misery. All those who took part in making Africa poor should also, in conscience, pay or open other avenues for the economic development of Africa to come out of age. If you do not want to do anything for us, our misery will overtake you. This is what explains the clandestine immigration. Laws, barbed wired border controls are good and enable all countries to affirm their national sovereignty. These measures will sooner or later become unnecessary when justice will be given to Africa. The late start of the continent must question more than one.

"The sanctions that we, the privileged cannot claim, those who suffer risk to impose them on us brutally. For, condemned she also knows everything, suffering humanity is starting to suffer for suffering. Knowing that the means exist that it does not suffer again, is will not tolerate to suffer indefinitely again."[9]

Nothing can stop our youth who suffer and dream of a happiness, nothing, not even failure in front of the barbed wire of Cueta and Melilla and even less the many brutal rebuttals and the brutal transit camps. Immediately sent back, they think of other ways to reach the same destination. The fantasy of a better life in the European Eldorado is too strong and continues to attract the youth in their thousands. If you do not stop the abject poverty here, then I will come to and make abject poverty visible at your home. One cannot

9. Abbé Pierre, *Op. Cit.*, p. 34

suffer infinitely and so the choice of migration becomes the better option and the only solution. Even if this can cause us our life, it is the only means to run away from the present misery. On 2nd October 2006, the day of commemorating the dead of Cueta and Melilla, others we said to have perished again. That same day, like celebrating a painful anniversary, other bodies, and since then every week young Africans lose their life in the Maltese, Libya, Italian ,Spanish waters and between the borders of Turkey and Greek. .

The memory of these young people is rarely mentioned like something to shameful to hide. This undignified situation should make us think because it is becoming disturbing. But by not mentioning it, African leaders and others elsewhere seem to find their salvation in silence. These youth are too quickly judged thinking that they deserve what they get because of their risky way they choose to migrate. What alternatives do African countries put in place to stop them from leaving? Without any noticeable improvement in living standards in Africa, this phenomenon will still exist in the world. As long as the majority of the people of the planet Earth cannot eat to their satisfaction, and to satisfy their thirst, and to have a decent housing immigration will exist.

Access to health is only within the reach of a minority few, leaving a majority of human beings to die of hunger, of thirst and sickness. Why is it that non assistance to Africans in danger does not constitute a breach of the law? Solving this scourge is not easy but to recognise it and speaking about it can open other perspectives of dialogue leading to some form of solution. Who are these migrants? Who is responsible for their mistakes? How can this suicidal journey be stopped? Is it possible to stop clandestine immigration of African in developed countries?

These are the points we shall tackle in order to speak about the issues of clandestine immigration. We shall analyse these questions, envisaging some ways and means to forestall the fact that hopelessness does not become the only refuge of the youth and that the precarious boats used by the immigrants do not also become the only alternative of run away from the continent risking the sea and the indifference of those who do not know hunger. In this essay, the problem of clandestine immigration is treated in such a way as to make the leaders of the continent to awaken to doing something to make success possible here in Africa.

Who are these immigrants?

To reply this question, this is what Francois Soudan, Abdallah Ben Ali and Laetitia Grotti, all of them journalists at *Jeune Afrique L'Intelligent,* wrote in 2005 after a research on the subject:

"Most of them are young (between 20 and 30 years), have been to school (60% of them have a High School certificate or baccalaureate) and forced to run away from their countries of origin by misery, political troubles, or the two of them together. And so, if Nigerians, Senegalese, Malians, Cameroonians and Congolese (DR) constitute the highest contingents, one notes that since 2002 there are increasing numbers of Ivorians mainly from the northern part of the country under the 'rebel' administration. A quarter of these clandestine are women of which most of them are pregnant or mothers of very young children; rape, unregulated prostitution or simply a wrong calculation (and illusory for that matter) that the presence of babies, born or to be born, will facilitate the admission into Europe."[10]

Between 20 to 30 years olds constitute the vital force of a country. This is the ages at which one tries his/her best to contribute his/her quota in the development of the various sectors of the nation. It is the age at which one tries to concretise the dreams and the projects of a lifetime. An old adage says that one is not at ease as when at home.

---

10. SOUDAN François et alii, « Clandestins, voyage au bout de la honte », in *Jeune Afrique l'Intelligent,* 16 Octobre 2005, p. 3.

Elsewhere, the insertion is not always easy. Humans always take some time to accept the other, especially when the other is seen as the invader, economic exile without any means and especially a prey to whom one can propose any type of degrading work and so subject to the taskmaster's drudgery. These youth do not hate their country but they are only hopeless seeing their dreams fall apart, without any future, like an ice cream in the heat of indifference of their leader. They feel they must go and try their chance elsewhere.

A journey made in shame with tears in the eyes, the African youth is bruised by the sword of the very ones elected to look after the common good. Everyone seems oblivious and nobody wants to do anything to improve the situation. The European mirage suggests to these youth that from the inside change is no longer possible. Africa is bleeding, she is empty.

These youth who finally succeed to set foot on the European soil are victims of what is called 'working in the black'. The patron is the master for he or she knows that a person without paper is a person without any rights. What is more, a 'person without paper' is a martyr under the pressure of the family still in Africa. Nobody wants to know how their son or daughter struggles to survive in Europe. All that others want from him or her is for him or her to save extricate the family from misery. When one has nothing for himself to survive in Europe, this pressure from the family in Africa is like a small fire at your back. Everybody has contributed something so that the young person can leave the hell of the country and now the European Eldorado has turned into vinegar. It is not the dreamt paradise for in Europe there are laws and regulations to be respected and followed. One must earn his or her bread from the sweat of his or her forehead and so our young person without paper and work is worried and falls into disillusionment. These migrants are our children who are crying out loud and clear their desire to see things change. At times when individuals in Africa exist only because they belong to an ethnic group or others, this therefore kills the being one self.

Who is to blame?

The blame is to everyone; to us African in the first place. Nothing is ever solved by always looking for the escape goat elsewhere. As long as there is corruption, favouritism and the praise of our bad leaders in the bid to get a favour we will be incapably to solve our own problems. Whenever shall we change from such mentality?

The blame is also to those who sell to Africa arms instead of helping Africa to build schools, hospitals and factories to transform the abundant natural resources. Even there, the blame is to Africa again because we can distinguish good from bad, we know very well that arms are used to kill while a school is the one which trains the workforce and the elite of tomorrow. Do we have the right to cultivate oppression in a land that knows so much evil: slavery, depopulation, colonisation, neo-colonialism just mentioning some few?

The blame is to our brothers who leave and do not come back. This is brain drain and of manpower. The blame is also and above all to our leaders who take egoistic advantage of the riches of our countries without preoccupying themselves with the poverty of the people. It equally behoves to our brothers and sisters in Europe who keep silent on what they go through there. When they come back home, they make others believe that life is easy in Europe. They quickly forget the difficult pain of exile, the small fortune gained through toil and self denials become a motif of pride once they come back home. What a complete change! That is why the youth are attracted to the developed countries.

The blame is to traffickers who gain their means of living through this dehumanising trade of clandestine immigration. They pack human beings in boats of fortune to take them across not to the desired Eldorado but to the mortuary and the grave.

The blame is on the youth themselves who take stupid risks to run away from the obstacle which is the imposed poverty without ever taking the risk of resisting and affronting the true difficulties they have. Ahmadou Kourouma said that a child does not abandon the hut of his mother because of the smell of the mother's flatulence. The fight for a better future must start from within. Africa cannot be saved without Africans. The savings which are misused in these journeys could have been used for other things for our countries, like starting agricultural cooperatives or starting a loan scheme...

Today the vital force of Europe is consecrated to its own development which is very good indeed. But why not follow this example in our own case and place? Why not create exchanges for knowledge and technology transfer? The blame for others; but where is our part on the contribution for the building of Africa? The changes are taking time to be realised. Do we have the patience to walk according to our pace? This is essential and vital.

How to put an end to this suicidal journey!

It has to be attributed to the government of the first generation whose priority is the future of Africa. The whole planet must participate in eradicating poverty, an epidemic of this continent, so as to allow Africa and other less developed countries to take off, to eradicate hunger and the lack of education. Hard work, construction of roads and working to make agriculture capable of satisfying our food needs. We have huge portions of land that are not put to use. Men and women of vision are indispensable for not only creating employment, but also to think about just and equitable remuneration of those who will give all of themselves in the building of this new Africa.

We shall come back to the future perspectives in our second part. Let us only note that, it is imperative for the youth to be involved in the building of this new Africa. Their future depends on it and so is that of their children. We are asking for debt relief for poor countries because they were given in conditions beyond the control of the majority of the youth of Africa and makes the economic takeoff impossible or difficult. Let us cut our financial coat according to our size rather than depending on others. Let us put into place policy strategies based on proper reforms. It is no benefit to use the eggs before they are hatched. Let us sanction by the ballot box those who take advantage of the collective resources for their own gain and good ignoring the vital necessity of others. Let us reach a certain maturity where the verdict of the ballot box is accepted in a democratic 'fair-play'. A concrete reality to admit is the respect of our constitutions on which Kä Mana wrote these words:

The Constitution has as main focus the definition of the fundamental principles of government and the common life, principles in the name of which any majority, whatever it might be, is legitimised and to which much comply. All problems that are seen in the life of any nation is therefore seen as judged, appreciated and resolved in the light of the principles already established in the Constitution, in the rationality of its choices and in the wisdom of its fundamental options....only, the Constitution is, to the extent to which it gives rules which allow altogether a balanced distribution of power, an efficacious functioning of political institutions which should be able to self-regulate and to mutual control without a huge split, the emergence of economic rules which limit the inequalities or do not accept that if it is for the improvement of the conditions of the weak and less privileged, in the promotion of a certain creativity and innovation in the sense of the common good[11].

In many countries of Africa today, it is not the duty of the leaders to conform to the principles already established by law, but to the ones which conform to their good pleasure.

---

11. Ka Mana, *L'Afrique va-t-elle mourir ?*, Paris, Cerf, 1991, pp. 159-160.

I.2. (The) Deep traces of Africa's past

The essentials of African culture have been transmitted orally by the past generations. To discover the episodes of the long past can be a very difficult task. Even if events have taken place in the past on the African soil, very few of them have been written in a credible manner. If we even know something about our ancestors it is because of this oral tradition of Africans (writing is not the only means of expression) and by the written history of prominent Africans of international standing like Joseph Ki-Zerbo, peace be to his soul, let us say rather that may the earth by favourable or light to him – this is a well known African expression.

In the central Africa we shall always be thankful to the eminent professors Elikya Mbokolo, Ndaywell and Achille Mbembe who never stop to remind us of the forgotten past. The knowledge of the history of Africa is indispensable to the understanding of the origin of (the) bleeding (of) Africa that we condemn today. The cut roots of the past are not allowing the African tree to grow to full maturity as other nations of the world. Not forgetting the eminent Africans like Cheik Anta Diop, Amadou Ampateba, Ahmadou Kouroma (that the earth may be favourable to them!) that we thank warm heartedly as well as others who researched that the continent may rediscover its soul! We have not forgotten them.

On the traces of these past two events our attention is drawn: it is about slavery and the slave trade of blacks on the one hand and colonisation of Africa on the other hand. These two points were raised by the young people who were interrogated during the research. But we cannot understand the past of the 'black' continent without first recalling the place of the ancestors in the life of our various societies. Our history does not start by the Atlantic slave trade. It is a big mistake to allow books of African history start by colonisation.

I.2.1 An overview of ancestral Africa

The ancestors, near to the creator God, are seen as the guarantors and the protectors of the living. They appear in dreams, and this is a positive sign of their continued existence on earth and their participation in their own perpetual memory. Their death is only a mutation and in some ways (already) the dead continue to exist. Louis-Vincent Thomas reminded us of the important role of the ancestors and their degree of participation in the social organisation of the living:

> *The ancestors, properly speaking, appear on a favourable day. They are after all, law givers and supervisors and as such they sometimes punish with cruelty (when men have violated the rules of the clan or have provoked disorder) and they reward rather (they become dispensers of riches, fertility, health and peace. Actually, if their vital force decreases (hence their death) they possess on the contrary as the Bantu say 'the force to know' (hence their intervention in the life of the living). Moreover, the power of the ancestors does not belong to them properly; it is indirect and derived; it comes from God. And so, they have prominent place and they can be situated between humans and the spirits or superior to the spirits or the divinities properly speaking[12].*

The ancestors are the respected members of the clan who lived commendable and exemplary lives and died according to the rules. They are intermediaries between the divinities and the humans. The prayers and cults that the living renders through them are of more importance than that of the fetish or small gods and marabous. Their actions are more important than that of the sorcerers who are on the fringes of society and whose main purpose is to destroy the group. The ancestors are the custodians of unity and the integrity of the group and they regulate the ceremonies and the different stages of life in Africa namely; childbirth, puberty, marriage, funeral rites... The living has to obey the ancestors for fear of calamities and reprisals,

---

12. THOMAS Louis Vincent, *Cinq essais sur la mort africaine*, Dakar, 1968, pp. 43-44.

but also to obtain their protection and blessing. Destiny and the finality of the communion of the ancestors are subject to and can take divers and varied significance. Nonetheless, one major idea goes through black Africa on the importance of the communion of the ancestors: it is about the consolidation of the collective conscience of the living so as to better struggle against death. Louis-Vincent Thomas expressed this or similar conviction as follows:

> Death henceforth considered as a destruction of the individual (and the appearance, that is to say, to reduce to the pure imaginary state), is found compensated by some beliefs which are more symbolic. Everything goes on as if the collective conscience, which is nourished by life, found in the world of the ancestors the reason for its continuity. Death can therefore be defined as the mediation of the individual towards the collection considered in what is the surest, the community of the ancestors[13].

All cultures of the world struggle in one way or the other against the fatality of death. Death is always a disaster whatever the case and whatever the age of the one who has died. Even in the developed countries where medical technology has made enormous progress and where life expectancy is still increasing, when death arrives finally everyone is distraught. Death in irreversible and what comes after is unknown: absurdity, nothingness, emptiness, a new life starts... Short, everyone goes according to his or her beliefs and convictions. Humans are capable of interpretation themselves and interpreting other things. Each person does it according to his or her desires, his/her beliefs and his/her knowledge. Death for an African is a dangerous nuisance that must be pushed far away and eliminated. To face death the Cartesian tradition resorted to science and medicine because for the Western mind death is a total destruction of the being. However, the African turns to life to forget the pain of death:

---

13. THOMAS Louis Vincent, *Op. cit.*, p. 125.

By a curious paradox, one can ask if western man fears death because he/ she refuses to believe in the power of life. On the contrary, the negro-African, - about whom it is known how rich and original, and with what enthusiasm he/she exalts life - minimises the reach of death in making of it an imagery which provisionally interrupts the existence of the individual being.: He transforms it into an event which has power only over the appearance of the individual, and so saves the social species (belief in the omnipresence of the ancestors, in maintaining the clan phylum/lineage because of reincarnation...)[14].

He faces in his own way the expansion of death. To the funeral rites, one thinks of the next child to be born who will take the place of the one who has just died. This is how for example Flavien Nkay Malu explained what it means to have a child among the Ding people of DRC:

According to the ancestral tradition, a child is the spirit of an ancestor (nsib) who entrees the womb of a woman, normally of his clan; it animates a new body which is born. This is the phenomenon of reincarnation that the eastern Ding calls usong'no. It is the reason why they give to each newly born child the name of the reincarnated ancestor. The Ding say that 'it is this person who has come back'[15].

Jean Paul Eschlimann also, who lived and studied the culture of the Agni people in Cote d'Ivoire (Ivory coast) underscores without reservation (that) with this people death-disorder is vehemently repulsed and replaced by death-new-birth (renaissance) with the mind that one must always think life in order to overcome death and chase it far away:

---

14. THOMAS Louis Vincent, *Anthropologie de la Mort*, Paris, Payot, 1976, p. 8.
15. NKAY MALU Flavien, *La mission chrétienne a l'épreuve de la tradition ancestrale (Congo Belge, 1891-1933)*, Paris, Karthala, 2007, p. 315.

Death strolls insidiously everywhere that there is life. It is co-extensive to life. Everywhere it does not have place in any village. The only thing that can be seen everywhere through festivals, rites, dances, games, reproduction activities, selling and buying, eating, through the many births and rebirths is life. As for death, it is constantly repulsed into dark and forgotten zones of the deep forest[16].

In Africa, life after death is understood and perpetuated by believes in the ancestral communion/community. All the negro-Africa social anthropology rests, as it is confirmed by Louis-Vincent Thomas, on the dynamic organisation of the vital forces:

The victory of life over death, the constant desire of the group to avoid the disorder, the continuity of the social phylum and above all the solidarity of the universe; that of the living and that of the ancestors; these appear to us as the main belief of the negro-Africans. They all rely on a philosophical understanding: that of the dynamic organisation of the vital forces[17].

But the attitude of the African towards death is still ambivalent since even if life must continue for some, others are also sanctioned by social death. All those who do not become ancestors because of their disordered aggressive behaviour towards the collective must die without leaving any traces and must be neutralised. Those who are not ancestors, those who are not welcomed by them are called to oblivion and must disappear.

Here comes the question: why is it that Africa which believes so much in life after death deprives some of her young people of a life after death? Who are those who incite the living to mistrust which is the origin of the sanction of oblivion? Which lessons can the living members of the clan learn from the severity of the sanction for those who cannot become ancestors?

---

16. ESCHLIMANN Jean-Paul, *Les Agni devant la mort*, Paris, Karthala, 1985, p. 29.
17. THOMAS Louis-Vincent, *Cinq essaie sur la mort africaine*, Dakar, 1968, p. 44.

In short, how can one understand the contrast between the African whose desire is to resist death through the ancestors and the same African who desires the social death and the exclusion or banishment of those who do not become ancestors or join them? We shall advance two hypotheses!

It is true that the celebration of life constitute the bedrock or backbone against the suffering that death can inflict in Africa. It is even truer that the manner and the quality of this life also count enormously! In this life, the elders must always give good examples to the younger ones. Analysing questions relating to life in African traditional societies Albert Muluma Munanga gave this overview:

> *Maurice Godelier, talking about the notion of traditional societies, recalls us to a range of customs and beliefs, the manner of living and thinking left by the ancestors. It appears as an aggregate of clan entities relatively far from one another by specific cultural orientations, the result of a range of ways which every local group impose on its members the beliefs that justify those ways, material objects associated with these beliefs as ways of life[18].*

One does not live anyhow in traditional African society. The opposite and the perversion of the social rules are not tolerated. Even if the ancestors continue to be part of the community of the living, the deviants among the living are harmful and must be neutralised. The harmful effects of their actions can be and are cause of profound trouble and disorder in the group. We shall try to advance two hypotheses to explain the sanction of social death:

*Banishment and exclusion, the sanctions of social death against an individual might serve to preserve the collective which in its soul is nourished by life. The perverse might be an obstacle to the vital force. Nobody among the living is expected to ignore this fundamental rule: the relationship of force between the living and the ancestors are regulated and normalised by the strict respect of

18. MALUMA MUNANGA Albert, *Sociologie générale et africaine. Les sciences sociale et les mutations des sociétés africaines*, Paris, L'harmattan, 2008, p. 173.

the habits and customs of each clan. Those who go against it put the group in danger and expose themselves to the sanction. This manner of treating the relationship living-ancestors which pass through the strict observance of the customary laws, I observed them in all the countries of black Africa that I visited. The Dagara of Burkina Faso would leave the son of a dead person to choose any branch of the tree to be sculpted and later planted in the sanctuary of the ancestors. This is the sign of their permanent presence. In my own country of DRC, one sees important civil servants and government officials come back to the village in order to implore the pardon of the ancestors by sacrifices and rites especially when nothing is going well in their work, in their marriage etc.... I can feel that the social realities of many Africans are divided between the influence of the tradition and the attraction towards modernity. This is the synthesis Albert Muluma Munanga made in the case of DRC in particular and Africa in general:

Africa ... is living at the crossroad of the past and the present where tradition continues to influence men and women of the 20th century who without despising the electricity that comes from the Inga dam, nylon and the airplanes, refers in some of their comportment to the clan to sorcerers, to fetish, to the extent that the separation between traditional and modernism is relative and uneasy! Despite their determination to redefine their colonialist impact, the authenticity that the societies look for is nothing other than the result of what it has from the past and external relations. The station of N'Sele for example is also found in N'Sele of DRC and not only at Houston of Texas in USA or Paris in France[19].

The traditional African society is, in the first place, a group which perpetuates, keeps and protects its identity. It ensures for everyone a

---

19. MALUMA MUNANGA Albert, *Op. Cit.*, p. 211.

place to be born, to live, to marry and to die. It remains a hierarchical society with communitarian structure: family, clan, tribe, chiefdom.

*Banishment or social death serves as caution and intimidation of the living so as to prevent the falling back into disgrace after their death as it is in the case of those who are not ancestors. The traditional society is sacred and draws the unity of its supreme values from the observation of the laws which unite the living to the ancestral community. This sacredness includes the norms which are not written; it includes common attitudes, ideologies, and instances of structures like customs, the ceremonies and usages. The control of the sacredness is based on the ancestral community. The living recognise the existence of this ancestral community which has the duty of assisting in every undertaken. That the laws are not written is given, but it does not mean anomie or the absence of social organisation based on laws, the power of the group is linked to the ancestors who constitute the foundation and origin.

These unwritten laws everyone is supposed to know them. In the oral tradition everything is passed on from mouth to ear through the taboos, things forbidden and totems of the group. In the western world one hears that everybody is supposed to know the law and the civil codes of the law can vary or differ from country to country. Those who violate these laws are liable to a fine or other forms of sanction prescribed by law. In traditional Africa it is a similar situation because all are expected to know the sacredness of the laws which unite the community of the living and that of the ancestors. The perverse undergo the severe sanction of social death or in some cases humiliation of being buried in the evil forest, of what Chinua Achebe of Nigeria describe in these considered terms:

> *Each clan and each village has its own evil forest. There, are buried all those who die through really bad sickness like leprosy or small pox. It is also the place where the fetishes of the important medicine men that died are kept. An*

evil forest is therefore animated by evil forces and forces of darkness (Things Fall Apart)[20].

Those who did not live dignified lives, which did not live exemplary life, are severely punished by the members of their own clan after their death. Through the evil forest, the target is the oblivion of memory. For Africans who keep direct content with the nether world this sanction is particularly painful. In France, it will be like depriving a loved one a funeral and a dignified tomb. I live in the small town of Barr in the region of Alsace and my house is just near the cemetery. No single day passes without someone coming to pay tribute to a loved one on their tomb. Some people bring flowers; some touch the grave stones ... In Africa on the other hand, those who are not ancestors are not supposed to be present in the memory of the living. They are deprived of the contact that the French have with their dead. Each clan, each village tries to obtain a good moral conduct from its members.

Another historical event will swing Africa's peaceful existence in the 15th and 16th centuries: it is that of the beginning of the Atlantic Slave Trade. Here opens a dark page which made the children of Africa victims of captivity in favour of economic gains of the West.

I.2.2. The Atlantic Slave Trade

My bitterness and dismay are great concerning this ignoble crime against humanity. The slave trade is an ignominy of human existence, a tragedy. In their books On Being a Slave (Etre esclave), Catherine Coquery-Vidrovitch, an emeritus professor and specialist in African history and Eric Mesnard a professor of History of Geography at Paris-Est University of Creteil situated slavery and the Atlantic slave trade between 15th and the 19th centuries:

---

20. ACHEBE Chinua, *Le Monde s'effondre*, Paris-Dakar, Présence Africaine, 1972, p. 179.

All along the 15th century with the exploration of the Western coast of Africa finished (1488 Bartolomeu Dias reached the Cape of Good Hope and opened from 1498 'the Indian Route'), there begin to develop progressively between Ceuta and the Cape a Portuguese-African slavery: thereafter with the 'discovery of America' by Christopher Colombo (in 1492) was put in place the geopolitical foundation of the European colonial transatlantic slave trade[21].

The period of the discovery of the Americas, from 1500 to 1750, there was huge increase in sugar cane plantations in the Caribbean of the north Atlantic. This period was accompanied by the generalisation slavery internal to the African continent which made the slavery of Black African its principal objective. This discovery of the America only came to aggravate the situation with the key feature of the making Black African inferior to the whites:

The discovery of America changed the situation. But it only with the systematic effort, across the Atlantic, if the plantation economy (tobacco, mainly sugar cane and later cotton in the United States) that the Negro slave system reached its apogee, from the end of the 17th century to the mid of the 29th century, creating the 'negro', that is to say the slave of colour tragically made inferior by the construction of the colour-bar[22].

Trafficking of Black African and later making their race inferior, four centuries have passed to the advantage of many protagonists: on the European side black African slave masters, bankers and sea captains with port of anchor at Nantes, La Rochelle, Lorient, Bordeaux, Lisbon, Liverpool and on the American side essentially plantation owners and men of politics. Four centuries during which was intensified a racial system which is fundamentally visceral

21. COQUERY-VIDROVITCH Catherine et alii, *Etre esclave. Afrique-Amérique, XVe-XIXe Siècles*, Paris, La Découverte, 2013, p. 25.
22. COQUERY-VIDROVITCH, *Op. Cit.*, p. 26.

or primitive, whose effects and ramifications have not totally disappeared. Of these slave cities Aimee Césaire wrote:

And I said to myself Bordeaux, and Nantes and Liverpool and New York and San Francisco not a single one of you who do not carry my digital print and my (calceneus) on the back of the sky-scrappers and my crass in the flicker of germs. Who can boost himself of having better than I? Virginia, Tennessee, Georgia, Alabama! Decaying monsters of inoperable revolts, wetlands of decaying blood, trumpets absurdly closed Red earth, bloodthirsty earth[23].

The history of the Atlantic slave trade, I was told in school very early and often without possible precisions, sometimes with the only aim of information that some of our ancestors were sold and reduced to nothing by the Westerners. Since my tender years, the simple mention of slavery and the slavery of blacks have always evoke in me a curiosity, a strong desire to quench a profound thirst in order to know the forms of exploitation which dominated ancient African societies, to try and understand first of all the history and the Atlantic slave trade dominated by the Portuguese and how it passed to the hands of the French, the British, the Spaniards and the Dutch. To understand in order to mourn and finally heal and turn the dark page of this deep wound on the African soul. This subject has always given me goose flesh and made me tremble within. I mention it in this book so as to heal and face the future. But how can one qualify this violent transfer of Africans from one continent to another Alphonse Quenum asked himself:

During four centuries and without interruption, the Christian world captured, sold, resold hundreds of millions of human beings. One qualifies as crime against humanity the murderous insanity of Hitler and his allies. How could one qualify this violent transfer of millions of human beings from one continent to another? These are questions which need to be asked. The

23. CESAIRE Aimé, *Cahier d'un retour au pays natal*, Paris, Présence Africaine, 1983, p. 24-25.

fact that those who were mainly responsible do not see any moral objection in treating as goods human beings – men, women and children, the fact that there was local accomplices to the slave masters caught up in the game of profit, could these facts serve as an alibi to the extent that historians would be disturbed to objectively qualify this phenomenon? It is not able rewriting history but to read it on the level of principles, of reasons of action, the major actors and the facts[24].

Here, it is about a crime orchestrated by the occupiers so as to make merchandise of the dominated people and to enrich themselves without scruple. Money often times has served as the nerve of the war and of inequality in the world. We cannot know all the facts of this shameful trade, but that does not prevent and stop us from digging, searching under heaven and earth so as to have an idea near to the truth. The truth one has to look for it, but it is found in the waves of the ocean, it is found in the sugar cane plantations of the Americas and the Caribbean, it is found in our African villages emptied of the vital work-force, it is in the common grave of the chained slaves, those who died of tiredness because of the long walks on foot, and it is found in the forgotten graves of those who died suffocated because packed as wood logs in compartments. It is in the ship wrecks, in the debris of the chains of Elmina castle in Ghana and on the island of Gorée in Lower Senegal, at Zanzibar (constituted a Sultanate in 1840 by the Arabs involved in slavery on the Indian ocean and the export of sisal, cotton and sugar cane). It is found in Haiti, in Jamaica, in Brazil, in Guyana, In Guadeloupe, in Martinique, in Guinea, at Point Noire, at Matadi, at Havana, at Ouidah, in Luanda, Benguela, Cabinda, ... Nothing except these last three ports of anchor in the 1640s more than 100,000 hundred thousand captives were send to Brazil ... It is found in the rhythm and the melancholic sound of jazz and black American gospels (negro

---

24. QUENUM Alphonse, *Les Églises chrétiennes et la traite atlantique du XVe aux XIXe siècles*, Paris, Karthala, 2008, p. 56.

spirituals), in the Cuban Salsa, in the songs of the Senegalese and Malian Griots. This music expresses the interior suffering of people abandoned to themselves and to their sad story.

The search for the truth is dear to me, in its silence it takes away part of my history. I am in search of it because in what it carries within is found the root of our so-called African-American brothers and sisters, of the uprooted blacks of Brazil and all persons of colour overseas who have lost a direct link with their ancestors. All the others in North America know how to trace their origin with certainty. We hear of Americans of Irish, Italian and French (especially in New Orleans) descents ... but for blacks who have passed from slave master to another might never know. In my opinion, here is found one of the ancient traces of cultural abnegation of the continent and people of African origin.

The silence around this subject hides the atrocities perpetrated by the slave masters and their heirs. This truth I am looking for it always not to judge the past with the eyes of today but rather to make peace with the present. When I let passion subsides to approach the subject with a step back and an informed consideration, I realised without wanting to spare the protagonists that traffic of such magnitude was not developed without an African complicity. This is an idea that Catherine Coquery agreed with when she wrote:

> *Slavery was practised for a long time by African societies including those situated in the heart of the continent and from this fact relatively protected from the larger international slavery currents to the west and to the east. Surely, slavery networks multiplied from the 18th century, but the widespread opinion is that up till that point many local communities suffered from the practice instead of participating in it. It seems however on the contrary that 'slavery was much more important than thought ... and that what is often affirmed, and that the role of African of the interior, those not on the coast, in the slave trade has been more complex and more important than what was*

thought. The hypothesis advanced is that 'the international dimension of the slave trade developed because it was already widespread in the region[25].

Let us leave the task to historians to establish the responsibility of each one, maybe they will tell us one day whether the local African societies participated in or are victims of the slave trade. There is a plausible hypothesis that such an evil would not have been possible without local complicity. Should it be an alibi to justify the evil of another? In my quest for the truth, I am looking for the smallest indication in books, in documentaries, at the cinemas...

The story book of the American Harriet Beecher Stowe which was made into a film entitled "The Case of Uncle Tom" profoundly disturbed me. This film gives the truth of the historical facts showing the extreme pain in the life of the slave: servitude, privation, reification. The slaves were employed to do everything. They worked essentially in the farm where they were harassed and severely underfed. The importance of the film is found in the fact that it has chosen to promote the right to be different and the acceptance of marginalised and dominated minorities. I visited some symbolic places which act as moving witnesses retracing the history of the slave trade: the Elmina Castle in Ghana (built by the Portuguese in 1486 and occupied by the Dutch in 1637, which became around 1500s a concentration camp for the distribution of slaves), the Gate of No Return at Ouidah in Benin, the Forts of Zanzibar in Tanzania and the museum of the slave trade in Nantes. The guides of all these places and the photos exposed plunged me into this macabre history. I could not prevent dew drops of tears to fall from my eyes.

I wept because Africa is bleeding today and her pains go back into history. I wept for my great grandparents who were taken away. I wept because, like myself, the African Americans whom I met on the same visit to Elmina could not hold back their tears. I have not taken part in this abominable trade neither were they since both, we arrived

---

25. COQUERY-VIDROVITCH et alii, *Op. Cit.*, p.23.

long generations after the disaster, but we felt similar anguish/distress as if the event happen only yesterday. In their groaning I read the bitterness and the hate because this has lasted in all four hundred years. I felt the same hate against those Africans involved, who in one way or another, have collaborated in this crime. I wept because, after the abolition of the slave trade, other forms of modern-day slavery continue to exist: forced marriages, the forgotten children who took part in wars and conflicts, child labour, child prostitution and human trafficking, the Blacks of Haiti disposed of everything at the border and who are forced to work in the sugar cane plantations of the Dominican Republic.

Again today, in Mauritania, not to mention only this country, human beings are born as slaves and live as such from generation to generation. I wept because true excuses and reparations are not forth coming: Africa bleeds because of this refusal! We cannot oblige anyone for these excuses; they have to come from the conscience of the colonisers. It will be difficult to turn this repressive page if today there are not efforts in the direction of equitable distribution of riches. We had to wait until 1990 for some African leaders to start claiming for reparation:

> *25 billion dollars! This is the amount Africa is demanding in reparation for five centuries of the slave trade. The request was officially made at the end of 1990 at Lagos in Nigeria during the World Conference for the reparation against Africa and Africans of the diaspora. Europe and the two Americas would therefore be debtors to a continent, one has to remember, is the zone of the world the most in debt (130 billion usd) in terms of gross domestic product. For the first time "The long night of the Atlantic slave trade" (according to the words of the former president of the Republic of Benin Nicephore Soglo) has found a formulation purely and coldly economic (monetary value). Africa is addressing herself to her former masters in their own language of numbers, the statistics (twenty million men and women 'taken' not forgetting the children to be born, the future workforce taken away from the continent),*

the result. What the western countries give us financial aid they should have given as what was due. Can Africa barter debts against the enslavement of Blacks? After all, defeated Germany in 1918 had to pay 132 billion Marks to the allied forces. Today again Mamadou Alpha Barry writes Germany is forced to pay compensation to Israel for the holocaust perpetrated against the Jews by the Nazis whereas this state did not existed at the time the crimes were committed. But the reparation could not erase the past, which will always be the past. The future with or without 25 billion dollars, we have to built it anyway[26].

I am not a staunch supporter of the reparation because 25 billion dollars will not erase the inner turmoil brought about by this crime except that symbolically it allows some relief of the pain of the soul as to reduce the lateness of Africa in the domain of development. When one suffers, nothing is more painful as contact with those who are indifferent said Laure Conan (Adolph, I-1816). What is important is the reconstruction of the dialogue of Africa and what is urgent is the reestablishment of the dialogue with her children dispersed. We would like that a true act of contrition is undertaken between Blacks,

26. FOTTORINO Eric et alii, *Besoin d'Afrique*, Paris, Fayard, 1992, pp. 58-59.

Blacks of Africa and Blacks of elsewhere, in the name of our own participation in this crime.

To re-establish the contact so that each one in his/her present milieu of life will remember Africa as his/her root. One day in a barber's shop in Chicago, Brown an African-American barber was making a joke that one day he would visit the jungle of Congo where polygamy is practised so as to marry many women. I told him it is safe however, if after a DNA test it is found out from the information of life tissues, that one of his future wives is from the same ancestor as himself. And there he started crying and telling me what he knew about the tragedy of the Atlantic slave trade of Blacks. That is how I was given a free hair cut. Those who were taken away and ourselves have the same and the only mother: Africa.

That this truth be said and taught to the children of 'Whites' today they are also strangers like us to this historical fact, but as a duty of memory let us talk about it. The traumatic experience is hurting us and scars still persist. This can explain (without justifying the abuses nor the responsibilities of Africa) the lateness of Africa in her development.

The youths interviews in the course of our discussions here and there on the African continent were right to have put the slave trade in the first position as the cause of the lateness of the economic development of Africa but this does not explain everything. I will say it again, for to justify our lateness by slavery and the Atlantic slave trade of blacks would be an easy escape and excuse. We shall establish the responsibility of Africa later. The scars of this dark page even though long time ago explains this de facto inclination towards resignation which makes of some Blacks to easily accept the fatality in considering themselves as sub-humans and to affirm the superiority of the White race:

In Europe, even half casts are Blacks whereas in Africa they are Whites. It is enough to cross the Mediterranean Sea to change one's race! This way of looking at half casts between Europe and Africa is due to the simple fact that in Europe anything mixed with Blackness loses its value whereas in Africa anything that is a little bit white gains value[27].

The past hunts the subconscious of some. The scars will continue to exist as long as Africa does not gain its economic independence. The African people have been maintained in slavery, subservient to degrading treatment and confined to force to do hard labour. The slave according to his /her condition, has confined to this inferiority his/her master and by contagion the same cliché are perpetrated by today's generation who are dependants of the past. The son inherits the culture of his father, the daughter that of her mother and the present is influenced by the past. Sadly enough today, some Blacks are convinced of their inferiority as against the Whites. This is the case for example, of some Africans in the diaspora in France even though government executives and respected intellectuals, accept because of want lack of better alternatives, subordinate and debasing works like garbage collectors, cleaners or watchmen a condition they will never assume or accept once in Africa. Equal chance for any employment does not depend on the qualification of the prospective employee, but sometimes and mostly from the origin of the employee.

With equal qualification the chances of getting employed are not the same:

France has practiced the choice for migrant workers the most segregated known in the West since the Atlantic slave trade. It is the case of the importation of the migrant workers for the works which the French are not willing to do. And in the scale of subordinate debasing employments the black African occupies without doubt the last place, after which those from the Maghreb in the automobile assembly plants and the mines and the small hospitals works who are from the Caribbean (West Indies) of BUMIDO. Such heritage after

27. KELMAN Gaston, *Je suis noir et je n'aime pas le manioc*, Paris, Max Milo, 2004, pp. 108-109.

the slave trade / slavery and colonization leaves deep traces, if not indelible, on our spirit[28].

The *subordinate debasing employments* are well catalogued and documented. Aimé Césaire gives us a sad description:

I want to confess that we have been from all the time the dish washers, the shoe shiners without scruple, putting things well, the better conscientious sorcerers and the only undisputed record we have broken is that of the endurance of the whip....and this country cried during many centuries that we are brutal beasts, that the pulsations of humanity stop at the doors of blackness"[29].

According to an order established since the slavery and the Atlantic slave trade, non valued and difficult jobs are reserved for the Blacks as in the past where places were reserved in a restaurant, in a concert hall or in a stadium. In this category will be placed harvesting and collecting in certain plantations, garbage collectors, gardeners, road workers, distribution of newspapers catalogues and advert leaflets .... I ask myself the same question like Kelman why is so much attention paid to the colour of my skin?

Is it because the colour of the skin of a man is more important than the colour of his/her hair? Is it that race gives an individual the specific characteristics which determines his behaviour for all eternity?"[30]

The scars are still present and when it is tolerated as it is the case, it becomes a norm and absolute value.

I would like to tell you what happened to me in 2006 at Lyon in France when I was in the company of a friend who is a French of the white race. Excuse me this detail because I have always understood that the greatness of a man goes beyond the consideration of his race (racial consideration). I wouldn't have mentioned this detail if not for the better understanding of my small story. Differences in

---

28. KELMAN Gaston, *Op. Cit.*, pp. 91-92.
29. CESAIRE Aime, *Op, Cit.*, p. 38.
30. KELMAN Gaston, *Op. Cit.*, p. 9.

skin colour are not the most essential thing in life: Let us remain in solidarity with what our common humanity gives us. The universal man is incarnated in the respect of the other. We have to go to what Alain Touraine calls "Today's Global Culture":

"To the global culture of today does not corresponds, no type of human being, no emblematic figure no more women as the men or the young and the old, no more the inhabitants of New York or of Paris as that of Rio or Kolkata. The destruction of social mediations have face to face with the globalization of the cultural domain and the (indispensable) multiplicity of social actors"[31].

This reminds me of the principle of cultural relativity (conference of Mexico 1982) which stated that each culture constitute both material and immaterial patrimony , bringing its knowledge of the world in enriching with the contact of others. Regarding my small story here is it: my friend proposed to my stroll on food on the shores of river Rhone. Did he want me to taste a good quality wine, a good wine of Bordeaux or Beaujolais Nouveau (New Beaujolais)? I don't know since it was meant to be a surprise for me. These were some lighted Boats docked which were renowned bistros. That was where my friend was taking me to. Two well built guards told him without seeing me, that the entrance fee was €10. But when they saw me, one of them said as a matter of fact: "here, blacks are not allowed to enter".

The face of my friend became pale for he could not believe his ears. He told the bailers that France is a country of law and that racial segregation was forbidden by the constitution. France one of the great nations in the world, the land of mode and style and haute

---

31. TOURAINE Alain, *Pourrons-nous vivre ensemble? Egaux et différents*, Paris, Fayard, 1997, p. 49.

couture and gastronomy rubs shoulders with people of anti-value like racism and the rejection of the other.

My friend suffered more than myself. I made him understood that even in Africa one can find some people who can say that they don't like whites. We cannot give way to discouragement because this would be an occasion for them to sing victory. Our true race is that of humanity and for it to be victorious, let us tell those who want to listen that the respect of dignity is sacred and that it has neither race nor gender nor age. Insults of racial character must be outlawed by the rigors of the law. Let us not always be on the defensive as those who are victimized. Let us embrace multiculturalism so as not to give way to "closed-ness".

Is the Blackman destined to suffer?

"Questions of this type are asked among the Blacks: would this have been a divine curse weighing on Blacks a curse which would have made the African an eternal subaltern? Is the story of Chan, the son of Noah a myth or a reality?"[32]

The black who is used to suffering, leaving for inheritance to the next generation only suffering, finished to believe that this is part of his destiny. I met many Blacks who made this state of affairs a credo of their life.

Things will not change let us therefore accept our misery and let us fight only to survive. That is why some of our doctors and (cadre) act as night watch and other small jobs because their destiny seems to them as all fatalism. The Black is not made to be a leader; his/her place is at the bottom of the scale/ladder of subordination. He has been (subalterne) and he believed the impossibility of standing with his head high. Aimé Césaire who analyzed this fateful condition of some Blacks gave this assessment:

They have put into his poor brain that a fatality weighs on him, that cannot be removed from his being; that he has no power over his own destiny; that a wicked Lord has written from all eternity laws of interdiction in his inferior

32. KELMAN Gaston, *Op. Cit.*, p.9.

(pelvienne) nature; and to be a good negro; to believe honestly his inferiority without any curiosity of verifying the fateful writings[33].

The Black is not destined to suffer. No! This is not our destiny. I would not believe in any such thing as fatalism the only absurdity is to permanently lower our heads and never to look up. Such a total resignation would open the way to inactivity and to stagnation. The only change will be to liberate ourselves from the heath of low self-esteem in which we closed ourselves.

The famous Jamaican singer Robert Nestor Marley alias "Bob Marley" invited us to free and emancipate ourselves from mental slavery. He was asking us to fight for our rights. I firmly believe that this is not weakness that we cannot overcome by the will to act in the right direction. What some people would wrongly call today destiny is nothing other than this mental slavery. The brain washing that made us accept this hellish inferiority imposed on us.

In North America, great efforts have been made in the sense of emancipation. Even if there is more to be done, we come to see that the fight of the Blacks like that of Martin Luther King is beginning to bear fruit. Everything is not yet done but the Black is not only a garbage collector. They occupy respected positions of responsibility in government and in business. One of them, Barack Obama, has become the President. Gaston Kelman regretted the slowness of the evolution of mentality on the French sides:

It seems unthinkable for a Black to occupy a good position in his / her work in France. However, if the figures of the 1990 population are anything to go by, after the South-East Asian community of the N'Guyen who are doctors or pharmacists of all strangers. Black Africans are the next of the highest population of managers and intellectual professionals. And I am talking of certificates of all those doctors or with university degrees in sociology or history and geography who for the men do gardening and for the women transformed to ward assistants in hospitals. To make sense of things, it must be said that

33. CESAIRE Aime, *Op, Cit.*, pp. 59-60.

it is among Blacks that we find the highest number of subordinate employments, of qualified workers[34].

To believe Gaston Kelman, a Black CEO of a large public enterprise will only shock public opinion and his/her presence will make a lower business turnover. If Gaston's interpretation is true, it will only be shocking to us that even today, a Black cannot be accepted but only as a subordinate and in no way in any position of leadership. The Black must fight to make this situation evolve, because it is not normal. Desperate by this situation which has become unbearable the Black Americans have protested and have seen that their situation evolved. It was therefore not their destiny; it is a negative perception which must be fought all cost.

There was in history of the world a people who had to face very difficult situations. We would like to establish some comparisons between the Alsatian tragedy and that of the Africans. Africa is not between two blocks (spheres of influence) as Alsace was between France and Germany but rather between our tradition and the western model. The pains and sufferings are not similar in our comparisons but at the end of the tunnel one has to assume his/her history and to advance giving oneself the means to work and never staying between two influences without ever becoming oneself. In Africa the failures on the economic, religious, political and social levels are easily blamed on slavery, the slave trade and the colonization of the west. Fifty years after independence, things have not evolved so much. Even the generation which did experience neither the slave trade nor the colonization find that the lateness of the continent comes from there. It is true that Black Africa has suffered so much. Her tragic history recalls slavery and the slave trade, the colonization and the neo-colonialism.

To use a concrete example, we live in Alsace where the people also knew miseries. In order to know what it is all about, readers are

---

34. KELMAN Gaston, *Op. Cit.*, pp. 90-91.

invited to watch the film *"Alsaciens"* or *"les deux Mathilde"*[35] : This film tells the tragedy of the people of Alsace between 1870 and 1953 where it was tossed between two cultures and two countries: France and Germany. Through the tragedies, the humiliations, the forced recruitments into the German army, the suppression of the French language to the advantage of the German language, the film director made us to understand that the Alsatians stayed French despite everything.

We have been staying in Alsace for some time now and wondered how much work has been done and how much the people have taken their own destiny into their hands even though this period of 1870 -1953 still remains in the memory of many. The reader will be aware that this period corresponds with the time of colonization of Africa and even then the Black still finds it difficult to assume the past.

He is still divided between two cultures. He wants to affirm himself as an African and at the same time live like Europeans. All the representation of his existence are disturbed and divided between the two. We are in front of a paradox: Africa is as the Congolese sociologist Albert Maluma said and already quoted, at the crossroads of the present and the past.

All the drama of lack of development on the continent is found in this divided behaviour difficult to understand. On the one hand, one can affirm having nostalgic of one's stolen past, on the other hand one is fond of western modernity. Up to what time can we justify our failures by the domination and the interference in our affairs by the west? The painful past which is not the prerogative of Africans is no longer the only excuse of our lateness in many domains. We have to stop playing the game of the victim of Africa. We must assume our condition by work and to advance into a better future.

---

35. This is a film of Michel Favart of 1995 in four episodes each lasting one hour thirty minutes.

The Alsacians have overcome their tragedy, why can't we do it then? To say that we are destined to suffer is to wrongly affirm that change is not possible. We cannot continue to look for our future in a tragic past imposed on us from outside. The present generations of westerners that we accuse have neither participated in the slave trade nor in slavery. All those we meet are not colonisers. Let us accept to move on despite new challenges to be met without doubt, we have to learn to question ourselves to accept our part of the responsibility in our failures and to invent the future by our work.

The pastor and stray elites will invite the people of Africa to be reconciled with her history. To evangelize to lead this people starts by helping them to accept, to go beyond so as not to be a subject of "between two" to become herself, to embrace Christ with his African heart and to face the challenges in the horizons. We cannot live without resisting the temptation of always accusing others; we cannot exist without inventing future perspectives and new avenues. We have most often tried to find in the past solutions to our present problems. Let us stop to believe that the simplistic politics of escape goats will bring growth to our economies. The theology of inventiveness of Jean Marc Ela and Leonard Santedi invite us to stir the soil and sow seed that will generate tomorrow.

Changing the face of our continent and our Church needs a great creativity and many inventiveness. Leonard Santedi explained in the following terms the effort which will animate this last part:

Henceforth, a delicate and dangerous but certainly urgent, important and vital task for future of Christianity on the African continent awaits the churches of Africa. That of thinking of an evangelization which takes the many challenges that the African peoples face into consideration, an evange-lization that affront straightforward the many evils overwhelm Africa today. In short, it is about an evangelisation whose main mission is to invent and to make appeal for invention for today and for tomorrow a new reply of the faith to the challenges of the history of humanity at the dawn of the 21st century. The credibility of Christianity depends on it[36].

The hour of inventiveness and creativity has come. The discourses have centred to long on the criticism against the slave trade and the colonisation and against the methods of implantation of the church especially Catholicism because the hand of the white coloniser is found in it. It will be necessary moreover, that the thinkers are capable one day to separate the misunderstanding between the colonial efforts and the evangelising mission of the church. A huge work has been done by the missionaries because thanks to their total dedication the Christian faith is no longer strange news in Africa and that cannot be forgotten. Many have paid the price of their lives to the evangelization of Africa.

There have been some mistakes of judgment concerning the culture of others. It is now the turn of Africa to leave the monotony of the discourses and to think theologically about concrete proposals in their scientific productions in order to face the challenges that face the Christian faith on the African soil. We cannot go on with this easy criticism without risking proposing new ways which will correct the mistakes of the past.

1.2.3. The Slave Trade and the Colonisation Are Intrinsically Liked

Has the Blackman been an object of conspiracy by the rest of humanity?

Allow me to respond in the positive to this question. Slavery and the Atlantic slave trade of Black came just after the discovery of the new world by Christopher Colombo in 1492. The slave trade and the colonization have a common denominator: the exploitation of the weak by the strong.

---

36. SANTEDI Leonard, *Les défis de l'évangélisation dans l'Afrique contemporaine*, Paris, Karthala, 2005, p. 9.

The colonisation is the necessary corollary of the slave trade: everything was going on through well-organised networks, the two becoming important issues of the policy of conquest. There was a real need for manpower since there was need for plantation farming and infrastructure of the new world. It is in the estimation of Catherine Coquery that:

The discoveries of the navigators of the 15th and 16th centuries were the points of departure for the European powers of the Atlantic for the colonial division and the exploitation of the "New World". On the American side, the "encounter" was followed by a brutal domination which led to enslavements, the disappearing of people and civilizations. Since his second voyage in 1493, Christopher Colombo came back as a colonizer with 1500 men among whom were his first slaves of African origin and plants to domesticate, of which is sugar cane: "After the Atlantic Mediterranean from Madere to the Canaries to the island of Cape Verde and Sao Tome, the sugar paradigm made the great leap to the Caribbean and the American following the great navigators[37].

A trafficking in humans started by this demand and that is why Portuguese, Spanish, French, English, Dutch not to mention the main actors who were launched into the operation of deportation of Blacks. We draw our evidence from the reconciliation and succession from these two historical facts: "the discovery of the Americans and the deportation of Blacks to the new continent. This thesis is defended by the great Senegalese thinker and historian Cheikh Anta Diop as it was reported by Gaston Kelman. The conspiracy of the rest of humanity against the Blackman is as a result of a long historical process of making inferior the black race:

It is at the beginning of this period that America was discovered by Christopher Colombo [...] the exploitation of the land necessitated man-power

---

37. COQUERY-VIDROVICH et alii, *Op, Cit.*, p. 93.

not too expensive. Africa [..] appeared as the obvious reservoir of humans already indicated where such labour could be fetched[38].

It is using second class human beings to inhuman ends like forced labour and trafficking. The Black deported, uprooted, disoriented has become an object in the hands of the master conspirators.

Would the complacent submission of Blacks have permitted these atrocities against them?

It is difficult to give an exact answer to this question. Can we talk about submission or complacency when we know that the means of resistance of the invading aggressors and the Blacks were not the same? The law of the strongest does not allow the Blackman any choice than submission. The Blackman had to accept in order to save his life. They preferred the chain, the bullying and the humiliations to death. Life is sacred in Africa and suicide is for bidden by tradition.

The images of chains are still alive until our days: to be chained is to be condemned to death. They wanted to make off the Black submissive creature forever. Still chained, the Black has continued to believe honestly that he is inferior borrowing the expressions from Aimé Césaire already cited. Nothing is worse than this sentiment of inferiority as against the other.

At the time of these events, submission was without doubt, the only recourse of the Black: to submit oneself or die. Without this disposition it will be difficult for us to explain why millions of Blacks were deported without any true resistance. What explains the submission is the violence that accompanied the slavery and the slave trade. Submission today is nothing but the complaints of the Black in his/her own auto-destruction. After the abolition of the slave trade submission of complacency became a serious problem to us. How can one understand today that the Black accepts easily this form of excessive abuse? Today more than ever, it is time to fight against this

---

38. KELMAN Gaston, *Op. Cit.*, p. 21

injustice. In his historical conception Joseph Ki-Zerbo considers that revolution have made this to advance.

Revolution is a structural process which makes things to advance invisibly up to the moment where, the significance of these structures is such that we must necessarily make a qualitative leap. I still take once more the case of African unity. Let us suppose that we still lack unity for another 50 years and that our problems have worsened to an epidemic level, of illiteracy, of lack of jobs etc. I am sure that groups within civil society would one day say: "this is no more possible, it is enough; too much, is too much" and they will access the general state of the African continent. It will be like in the night of august 4, 1789 during which the French constituent national assembly voted to abrogate the last privileges of the nobles and the clergy. It will also be a revolutionary act like the very moment when Jean Sylvain Bailly, who presided this memorable national assembly in the famous "Salle du jeu de paume" (the Hall of the Tennis Court) on behave of the third estate said: "the people gathered cannot receive orders". It is not only turning the page but also change the dictionary[39].

The Blackman can no longer play the game of complacency and submission, the stagnation and the inaction are equivalent to complicity, docility and the approval of fate. The one who says nothing agrees – silence mean consent. What has to be envisaged here is neither consent nor abstention. The duty to react is an evident urgency. To say no to the inertia, this is the revolution. Faced with Africa bleeding we must act by a non-violent and an uncompromising in submission (in subordination) the Black wounded by repressions and disaster must start his resistance today. He must revolt against these who still continue to take him as less human (sours home). During his time, Jean Rostand had foreseen, and justly so that: "there

---

39. KI-ZERBO Joseph, *Op. Cit.*, p. 16

is no suffering comparable to the sentiment of natural inferiority complex" (Ignace ou l'ecrivain-1923).

Non-violent insubordination, because as it was said by Martin Luther King, violence is as ineffective as immoral. It is not effective because it starts an unending circle of violence that can lead to total destruction. Yes it is true that violence leads to total destruction. All the rebellions insurrections in Africa have succeeded only in planting insecurity in the population: horror, terror, violence, genocide, violation of rights and impunity of perpetrators. Our rebellions with deep wounds (refugees, displacements, separations, famine, lost of work, lack of schooling, exploitation) push us to reorient our fight towards a nonviolent resistance. In other parts of the world, violence has led to atrocities and to horrible desolation.

The civil war cost one million dead to Spain, one million also died in Mexico – "la violencia", this type of civil war that resulted in nothing not even in dictatorship, made in Columbia 400,000 dead for a population which is only a quarter of that of Spain or Mexico. Mexico always remembers her revolution as Spain also does, as Columbia also does. We don't want any more"[40].

We would like that things change inviting the Black by the most possible peaceful means to contest this injustice. Violent gives birth to violence. The fight for equality of rights concerns all of humanity, her nobility necessitates without waiting our resistance. Our managers should no more be happy when they are made inferior and reduced to works of agriculture, of working in hotels restoration and public work. Without minimising these sectors, we don't want anymore that painful, less attractive and sociably degrading works be the privilege for the African in the diaspora. All Black people dispersed through the world should act in order to turn round the

---

40. LARTEGUY Jean, *Les guerillos, Jean Lartéguy sur les traces de Che Guevara*, Paris, Presses Pocket, 1967, p. 222.

tendency of a falling destiny. What Aimé Cesaire said in an interview to Le Monde newspaper is very significant:

> *"Like Senghor, what is common to us is the tenacious refusal to be alienated, to lose the attachment with our roots of origin, our people, our languages. Moreover, in my case, what preserved me to a large extent culturally is the constant visiting of Africans. This contact was a sort of counter balance to the influence of European culture. Senghor with whom I have lived almost ten years in the Quatier Latin before the war exercised a considerable influence in my personal universe. Like him, I did all that it takes to assimilate but not to be assimilated. One or the other, we are francophone, acquired the French culture, but for the miraculous weapons we want to put them at the service of our people[41].*

Contacts between all black people dispersed throughout the world are even more discernible so as to recreate the links broken by history. The Blacks of Africa in addition to this should reverse the democratic, economic, and food declines. Health, education, transport, sports, the state of the roads and employment should not be put away in file cabinets in our ministries. It is necessary to start from now to constitute priority areas. Instead of being foolishly afraid, said Abbé Pierre, let us be on the lookout for what is practically possible. We shall come back to a large extent on the future perspectives in our second part.

History thought us that on December 1st , 1955 in the United States, during the time of Martin Luther King, a black woman tired of paying a submissive fame, Madam Rosa Parks[42] , this pioneer of the fight for civil rights, refused to give up her place to someone

41. CÉSAIRE Aimé, "Interview par Philippe Decraene", in *Le Monde*, 7 December 1981.
42. Rosa Parks was born in 1913, a black woman who refused to give up her place to a white man in 1955 at Montgomery (Alabama) in the south –east of the USA. Her action will result in the abolition of racial segregation in 1964. She died at home in Detroit (Michigan) in the north east on Monday 24th October, 2005 at the age of 92.

of the dominating race, a white man. There is no pleasure at all in playing forever the submissive game subject to the dictates of others. We have to act in order to establish the equilibriums to come back to equity (equality) and to be respected.

La Porte du non-retour – the gate of no return[43]

For the slaves, the crossing was a terrible separation because it means almost certainly that they will never come back[44].

---

43. This gate was built during the commemorative celebrations in Quidah 1992, which was a moment of huge return on the traces of the past kingdom of Dahomey and those who were taken away during European slave era which lasted between 16th and 19th centuries, and cost the life of more than one hundred million deportees from Africa. This monument was built in memory of the millions of Africans who paid with their freedom and even more with their lives to the edification of the economic power of Europe as well as the fortunes of some nobles in Bordeaux, Nantes and elsewhere.
44. COQUERY-VIDROVITCH Catherine et alii, *Op. Cit.*, p. 92.

During my visit to past historical sites which bleed Africa, I was not animated by the same curiosity as that of the European tourists who are happy to have discovered a new place planning their holiday. I have seen hundreds admire the fantastic wildlife of Kenya in the Masa Mara Park where rare animal species are protected. I have seen them at Amboseli at the border with Tanzania their eyes towards Mt. Kilimanjaro, the highest mountain in Africa, wondering at the snow cap top and the beautiful sun set.

At the gate of no return the discovery was rather sad. Here, this lost memory came back to me. As the name indicated, they went and never came back like the dead who cannot come back to life. The slave trade invaded my thoughts; my feet were standing on the very site of the crime itself. Bitterness and deep pain occupied my spirit. Marcus Rediker a professor at the University of Pittsburgh in Pennsylvania in the USA a specialist in trans-Atlantic history gave us the daily life of slaves on the slave ships across the Atlantic Ocean. He spoke among other things about this woman.

> *The story of this woman is nothing but an act of what the great researcher and African-American militant W.E.B. Du Bois once called "the magnificent drama of the last thousand years". That is "the deportation of ten million human beings from the dark beauty of their mother continent towards the all new Eldorado of the West. They descended into hell". Taken away by force from her native land, this woman was put on board a ship which was to take her to a new world of work and exploitation, a world where she will probably be farming sugar cane, tobacco or rice so as to make her owner rich*[45].

This is the story of deportation, a terrifying journey which forced millions of blacks to confirm themselves to the extreme violence of chains and fortunes of their future destiny.

This gate of No-return is found on the shares of the Atlantic Ocean on the beak in Ouidah in Benin. This monument symbolizes

45. REDIKER Marcus, *A bord du négrier. Une histoire atlantique de la traite*, Paris, Seuil 2013, p. 13

the shameless traffic which is the slave trade, this organized crime where millions of Blacks were deported by slave traders to the exploitative end. This gate calls to mind the forced displacement of human beings of the 'black colour' to unknown places and as the name suggests, they did not return to their own native land:

In the 16th century started the external invasion; a sizeable interference with the "great discoveries" of Africa south of the Sahara and Latin America., these discoveries entailed, as you know, the slave trade. After the Indian genocide, the slave trade has cost the lives of tens of millions of Africans who were taken by fore from this continent and sent in atrocious conditions over the ocean. No groups of human beings have been inferiorized as Blacks after the 16th century.

Black slaves were ordered in millions: Blacks were used as means of reproduction of other blacks for the works on the plantations. How many African children were thrown overboard ships or abandoned in forts far away from their mothers who were taken, because it would have taken too long to look after them before they can be exploited? They were bought in tons. They amputated and butchered as meat the rebellious one who were called 'brown Negros'. During this time theologians in Europe were discussing in a learned manner the questions of whether Blacks have a soul. This is a question which was not asked in the case of other groups of human beings. All this is known and nobody can deny it.

But how is it that we have not been able to recognize that all of humanity has been made inferior, humiliated, sacrificed by such treatment? The slave trade of Blacks is the turning point of making-time, of trampling, and the stopping of African history. I have not said of history in Africa, but an inversion, of a reversal of history in Africa. If we ignore what happened through the slave trade of Blacks, we don't understand anything about Africa[46].

---

46. KI-ZERBO Joseph, *Op. Cit.*, p. 23.

They have left as salt dissolves in water in a cooking pot. This death affects Africa at her very core and her soul, she who has lost a part of her children. Children of the family are dispersed one at Nantes, at Rochelle, at Bordeaux one other of the United States of America. They change masters, from hardship to servitude and between brother and sister in Nantes, those in the USA and the rest of the family in Africa. Silence and tears are the unique link. Today Africa does not weigh heavy among nations, it weighs but the economy is very weak. They quickly forget the contribution of her departed in the edification of the economic power of Europe and America. Ki-Zerbo is one of those who claim the contribution of African in the industrial boom of Europe and the United States of America.

By the slave trade of Blacks and slavery, Africa has contributed to propel industrialization of Europe[47].

Like that the misfortune of some can sometimes be the happiness of other. Some say life is (nothing) not worth it if one cannot go to the end of his/her dreams. My dream is not only to write but above all to see the world reconciled with Africa and Africa with the rest of the world. That all the ends of the world which hold the black digital print (black fingerprint) hold high the head and turn definitely this page without bitterness. Jean Rostand said: "each suffering holds within it its grudge". I don't want to follow him in this way, I would rather want to hear Gaston Bachelard say to us:

Suffering is always linked to redemption a joy of the intellectual effort[48].

One cannot keep quiet on the truth. We cannot allow the assassination of the truth. Our conscience is still suffering from it. We have been victims of the logic of profit, reification, and emptied of all honour. I write to patch back the bits and pieces, the worries,

---

47. KI-ZERBO Joseph, *Op. Cit.*, p. 23.
48. BACHELARD Gaston, *L'intuition et l'instant*, Biblio Essais, 1932.

the debris, the shards and not the bottles, but from my story, from my existence, from my soul, of my people. I write because I believe in Lumumba, in Nkrumah, who asked as to re-write the history of Africa to be able to finally mourn our departed brothers and sisters. They have left our shores far away from us and the slave masters sold them out like object, lime animals. The American writer Harriet Beecher Stone recount the sale of Black at auctions whose prices go up according to any expertise [extract from South Carolina (Columbia) of 4 December, 1852]:

> "*Following blacks will be sold on Monday 6thDecember at the price attached to their names. Andrews, 24yrs old, a mason and plasterer, an accomplished worker; George, 22 years of age, the best barber in the state. James 19 years, an excellent painter. These young men were taken from Columbia and they have exceptional qualities and are put on sale without being accused of any fault*"[49].

The runaway Black has truly suffered humiliation, animalized, reified and sold. To change masters the Black merchandise cross the border from Latin America to North America. Their masters without money have to sell their slaves. Their names are changed according to their new master. Some took the huge risk of escaping so as to liberate himself from the cruel treatments they undergo:

> "*500 dollars in compensation - A handsome mulatto between 21 and 22 years old and called Wash has escape from the undersigned on 25th May. The said mulatto, on close observation looks like a white, because he has a light skin, he has blond hair, blue eyes and beautiful teeth. He is an excellent mason; but because of fear of being discovered, according to all probabilities, he will not continue to exercise this profession. Despite these extras, which assimilate him with the white, he has all the dispositions of a Blackman, takes pleasure in singing comic songs and cracks jokes. He is an excellent housekeeper who will do marvels serving in a hotel. He is tall, slim and lowers*

---

49. BEECHER STOWE Harriet, *La clef de la case de l'Oncle Tom*, Adamant Media Corporation, p. 25.

his eyes especially when one speaks to him; he sometimes has excesses of temper. He will without doubt be employed by someone miserable, and I will give this compensation to anyone who will retake this mulatto and reveal the thief, and who should be delivered to me at Chattanooga. Or even I promise 200 dollars for the mulatto only or 100 dollars only if he is put in prison in the United States, in a manner that it will be easy for me to go and take him back. George O. Ragland, Chattanooga, 15 June 1852[50].

The aim of the Atlantic slave trade was to remove the culture of the individual which is manifested in dehumanisation made possible by the loss of name and language. Even when the masters abuse the black slave women to satisfy their libido, the white blood loses any value because of its mixture with a black blood. The mulatto fruit of this union, suffers the same humiliations as blacks. Oh back blood which crime have you committed!!! Instead of condemning the mulattos, these whites would have desisted from bringing them into the world. Why have they humiliated themselves by having sexual intercourse with people they consider as of the inferior race? A slave mulatto is nothing but the irrefutable evidence of dichotomy of their cheating. One brings a child into the world to reject him/her later on enslave him/her is that not infanticide? But how can there be a dichotomy between beings which have a common humanity? This song composed about five thousand years by a Vedic poet and reported by Edouard Schuré is of a great conscience and breaths our common humanity;

"The (sky) heavens is my father, he beget me. I have as family all the celestial entourage. My mother is the large earth. The highest point of her surface in her matrix; the father gives fertility to his own by the one who is both his wife and his daughter."[51]

50. BEECHER STOWE Harriet, *Op. Cit.*, pp. 24-25.
51. SCHURE Edouard, *Les grands initiés, Saint-Amand, Librairie académique* Perrin, 1960, p. 31.

Peaceful coexistence between races of opinion and beliefs are a necessity. They have limited the capacity of the Blacks to certain domains: singers of comic songs (refrain), those who tell or crack (silly) jokes... These received ideas would be taken up and become in our days a profession of faith. Gaston Kelman castigates this erroneous perception of the earl of Gobineau on Blacks.

> "The Earl of Gobineau affirmed that the Black is made for art as the monkey is made for a life on tree tops and grimace or wince. For the Black there is need for sensuality and for the agility and dexterity of the monkey. But as both do not have intelligence, they have to submit themselves to a master who will canalise their gift in order to make it presentable in a tour of circus. In addition to this destiny of an entertainer, the Black sees himself or herself denied of any capacity of conception (thinking) and reflexion. All success of the black is rationalised and brought to the sphere of nature and so of bestiality. Neither the sociological conditions nor the individual efforts were taken into consideration, if he/she succeeds in sports. It is because of his aerodynamic morphology and his/her muscular mass.
>
> For music and the rhythm, he/she has it in the blood. However, if the choice has not been made to bestialise the Black, we would have easily understand that the morphological predispositions or the blood alchemies have nothing to do in his/her performance, but rather a banal necessity of adaptation to his/her environment, (an obligation to services) a bond of survival, just as there are more skiers in the Alps than Paris or in Conakry. If we take the case of Sports, it is evident that the negro-Americans have become great champions to the entertainment of whites, in the same way as the gladiators jumped into the arenas to confront the lions or a human enemy, to the joy of Creaser. On the subject of African Americans it turned out quickly that the distraction of the master by sports was one of the rare ways to bring success fortune and notoriety[52].

---

52. KELMAN Gaston, *Op. Cit.*, pp. 141-142.

Everything has been put in place to degrade the black born without intelligence, without any sense of initiative. Even his/her successes are simply attributed to his/her morphology and to his/her animal nature. There is a unanimity about his/her inability to carry out any logic, reasoning. His/her ability in cracking jokes and singing has been recognized. He can sing like the cock, the cicada, the nightingale and cracking jokes like a monkey. This is the level to which he is reduced to for some all indications are that these preconceived and propagated ideas are true. The partisans of white supremacy continue freely to adhere to these gossips and idle talk.

I.3. Colonisation

"In Europe, the thirst for the African territory was henceforth palpable. Some conflicts claim have to be calmed, and the need to manifestly establish some basic rules so as to divide the African continent. Bismarck proposed to hold a diplomatic conference in Berlin destined to discuss the problems. On November 15, 1884 representatives from the European powers sat around an iron round table facing the garden of the official residence of Bismarck in yellow bricks on Wilhelm Street. Among the ministers and plenipotentiaries in official costume and who took part under the vaulted plafond and glittering chandeliers are Compts, barrens, colonels and a representative of the Otto-man Empire. Bismarck who was in a colourful costume welcome them in French, the diplomatic language. Sitting in front of a large map of Africa, the delegates started their work[53].

Just a dozen years after the abolition of the slave trade, they the (English, Freeh, Portuguesa, Spaniards, Belgians and Germans) found another means to continue the domination of the Dark Continent. Let us not denounce too soon the Berlin conference which organised the formal partitioning of Africa and the colonial expansion methods with the arguments of today. The long quotation of isidore Ndaywel-

---

53. HOCHSCHILD Adam, *Les fantômes du roi Léopold. La terreur coloniale dans l'Etat du Congo 1884-1908*, Paris, Édition Tallandier, 2007, p. 147.

è-Nziem shows on the contrary how the participants seem to have a good faith:

"The Berlin conference had lived. During the following years, the conference had acquired a repercussion that it did not have earlier. It became evident, mostly because, of the interest in this chapter of the readings proposed by African history either by G. Hardy (1922), of Ch. A. Julien (1942), of H. Deschamps (1952), of R. Cornevin (1956-1964), of Ganiage (1968), of H. Brunschwing (1961) or of J, Ki-Zerbo (1971). In Africa one came to know through the attention that was accorded the centenary celebrations in 1984-1985.

This sufficiently shows the high significant character that the contemporary world attached to this historical event. However, even if there is a common understanding on its historical importance, its precise content has given rise to different and divergent interpretations. The first disdain to be revealed is the fact that even if this event is seen today as condescending or deprecatory the contemporaries of the conference and its participants had no bad conscience. On the contrary, they were proud to have accomplished a beautiful endeavour, good from all points of view, for Europe and for Africa[54].

It is true that the context is not the same and we have to free ourselves from easy and cheap criticism. An effort to link with the mentality of the time can help to understand the chain of events basic to the functioning of the colonial system. What is scandalous today was a motif of glory in the time of the conference. Isidore Ndaywel wrote again:

The Newspapers of the time do not hesitate to show this motif of glory as witnessed by this article in the Belgian Independent of March 2, 1885: The ships can now come and go freely on the seas around this zone of three million square kilometres [...] the workers that our old land can no longer feed and who do not have any work than to manifest their lack of work, will find

---

54. NDAYWEL-è-Nziem Isidore, *Histoire du Zaire. De l'héritage ancien a l'âge contemporain*, Louvain-la-Neuve, Duculot, 1997, p. 278

there a land of hospitality where they will exploit ivory, rubber, cereals, all the resources of these fertile region under the protective eye of civilised states whose boarders are now regulated, whose liberal laws are guaranteed in their functioning[55].

It is seen that the enthusiasm of the partitioning of the African cake is welcomed by the colonisers who can finally turn round their jobless curve and to exploit the resources of the African continent freely. For us, this is a consequential reading of the tragedy. For the so-called civilised nations, on the contrary, the conference of Berlin was a useful bet but Ndaywel went farther:

One can denounce the false role that the different interpretations came to play that the conference should not have formally partitioned Africa, not laid the principle of sphere of influence, not even recognise the EIC which has acquired a sort of "international colony" status (Stengers J., 1986: 11-19) it still remains true that Berlin would constitute the point of departure, the putting in place of a colonial expansion method which saved European powers from conflict; Berlin appears as the first attempt of a "Society of Nations" where the first international convention s were concluded that was not the result of a war (Chambard L., 1985: 19)[56].

From the African point of view the Berlin conference represent a bad news which established sometimes incomprehensible barriers between friendly neighbours. Some of those who pride in the goodness of colonisation have never explained to us the real reasons of this system. If there is any benefit would it have been compared to the repression and the plundering of the resources and the exploitation of a whole people? Adam Hochschild describes here

---

55. NDAYWEL-è-Nziem Isidore, *Op. Cit.*, p. 278.
56. *Idem.*, pp. 278-279.

the colonial terror that the Belgian king Leopold II used to rule the state of Congo:

"On examination today of the written and photographic testimonies one could not but to ask this crucial question: how many were the exact victims of the regime of Leopold in Congo? The moment has come for us to interrupt our expose and to try and to find an answer. The question is not simple. To start, it is not possible in this case to define a precise historical framework, as it could be done for example to determine how many Jews were killed by the Nazi between 1933 and 1945. The independent state of Congo, personal domain of Leopold II, has existed officially 23 years starting from its creation in 1885, but many Congolese were dying from non natural causes before the start of this period, and the essential elements of the exploitative system put in place by the Belgian king were still perpetrated for many years even after its official end. The rubber boom which was at the origin of the worse massacres in Congo, started in the middle of the 1890s under Leopold's administration but continued for many years to the end of his autocratic regime"[57].

Before one speaks frankly of any goodness of the colonisation it will be better to reflect and to ask the question of the meaning of these massacres and why having scourged the African continent in making so many victims? We can never put in the light the number of victims of the draconian systems judged also negligible as one forgets to have shaved his beard in the morning:

"The list of known and documented massacres is unending. The territory was covered with dead bodies, sometimes literally. At the place where a stream enters the Tumba Lake, E.V. Sjöblom a Swedish missionary wrote, I saw [...] floating on the lake dead bodies with their right hand cut off; on my return the officer told me why they were killed, because of rubber"[58].

---

57. HOCHSCHILD Adam, *Op. Cit.*, pp. 373-374.
58. *Idem.*, pp.376-377.

71

King Leopold II was not the isolated case in the abuses on the continent. Hochschild reported such cases elsewhere:

"The truth on the Congo publicised many articles relating to subjects like 'The opium of the British India' and press releases showing the bad side of the British Empire pain of beating with cords and whip in Southern Africa, human sacrifice in Nigeria, different exactions/extortion in Sierra Leone"[59].

This was the ain of the people during the colonial era. One disaster chases another one; after the slave trade, the colonisation. The main actors were more concerned with going to the end of their plot. They brilliantly succeeded in their plans: always to exploit and to use the resources of Africa. The funeral dirges of Blacks continue and Africa is divided into several parts and that is why we would like to sing, listen to our (griots). They say nothing but only that. They speak of the sadness of the African (black) soul. Humour is our only defence; we need it to struggle against the hopelessness of an Africa that is bleeding. Silence has become our only strength so as to digest this evil and to look for understanding. One keeps quiet when suffering becomes routine and a way of life. At a certain point the sufferings of Rwanda, of Darfur, the dead of the war in eastern Congo do not choc any longer.

The news papers are tired of reporting what has become banal and a common place event, only some more dead. In the examples already mentioned, the international community only reacts when it is too late. The Blacks are left to themselves to kill one another and to bury their dead first. After all, they are only Blacks and for what reason should there be any hurry to help? Humour, songs and silence are the coping mechanisms to digest and overcome our suffering which comes from afar, and you know it.

For many thinkers, the slave trade and the colonisation do not have any motivation except that of satisfying the aspirations and

---

59. HOCHSCHILD Adam, *Op. Cit.*, p. 394.

the economic endeavours (escapades) of the West. We have not yet found any other motivation than that:

"As regards the immigration of the workforce, certain historic occurrences (detours) should make us to think. The different forms of servitude under which the Blacks go through since the slave trade could not have been the work of chance. It is particularly troubling to note that the colonisation efforts started in Africa only after few years that the transatlantic slave trade of blacks was really abolished. For many observers and according to the sayings of the blacks themselves, the abolition of slavery was not due to humanitarian reasons and concerns. It was due to the banal economic logic that the trade is too expensive and regards the benefits derived from it. And then colonisation started"[60].

Since the slave trade and slavery, the life of Blacks has been desecrated in the interest of economic gains. Money is more important that the life of the Blackman. The logic of profit has its roots in the slave trade, its stem and branches in the colonisation and its scars still exist to date. This logic has de-accelerated, trampled and stopped the history of Africa. It has most of all dehumanised the Blackman. We have tried to find some attenuating circumstances to the colonisation. I was uncomfortably surprised to see the French parliamentarians debating the civilisation mission of colonialism. Stop to make mockery of a whole continent. You can call it whatever you want, but for us colonisation equals: exploitation, deprivation, reification, maltreatment, dehumanisation, slavery, alienation, manipulation, assimilation, bestial servitude, lowering, humiliation, invasion, interference, and discrimination. For Ki-Zerbo, the colonial system was a 'hold-up', disfiguring of Africa so as to make it a property:

---

60. KELMAN Gaston, *Op. Cit.*, pp. 41-42.

"Colonialism was a system which was used to replace entirely the African system. We have been alienated, that is to sat, replaced by others including our past. The colonisers have prepared a hold-up on our history. The 'Colonial project' wanted Africa to produce only raw materials to be sent to the north for European industries. Africa itself has been stabbed, divided and this role is placed on her: provide raw materials. This colonial project continues until now. If you take the trade balance of African countries you will see that 60%-80% of the value of exports of these countries comes from raw materials. For some of the countries it is copper, for others it is bauxite, uranium or cotton. When with Kwame Nkrumah, Amilcar Cabral and others, we fought for African independence they told us: 'You cannot even produce a pin, how do you want to be independent?' But why was it that our countries cannot produce even a pin? This is because during hundred years of colonisation this role was decided for us: not to produce even a pin but only raw materials, that is to say, to rob a continent. On the continental level Africans were mobilised for a 'noble struggle'. I am not talking of the dirty colonial wars where they were using us against others – in Vietnam, Algeria, Madagascar and elsewhere. During the first and second world wars, our brothers, our sister, our parents participated in the struggle against Nazism and fascism. We contributed as human beings in the defence of the sacred principle of human dignity"[61].

On July 26th, 2007, President Sarkozy whose hyper activism and concern for the revaluation of work, confessed that colonisation was a serious fault, this evil has brought the plundering of Africa.

But how can President Sarkozy confess the evil of colonialism and to refuse at the same time to repent? Only he can give the true reasons. But we do not understand how one can recognise having done wrong to others without wanting to say sorry. Here is the whole

---

61. KI-ZERBO Joseph, *Op., Cit.*, p. 24.

of the speech pronounced on the evening of July 26, 2007 at the Senegalese capital of Dakar:

"Ladies and gentlemen [...] I have come to talk to you with the frankness and sincerity that one owes to friends that one appreciates and respects. I appreciate and respect Africa and the Africans.

Between Senegal and France history has woven ties of a friendship that no one can undo. This friendship is strong and sincere. It is for this reason that I wanted to address, from Dakar, the fraternal greeting of France to all of Africa.

This evening I want to address myself to all the Africans who are so different the one from the other, who don't have the same language, who don't have the same religion, who don't have the same customs, who don't have the same culture, who don't have the same history and yet recognize the other as being African. Here one finds the first mystery of Africa.

Yes, I want to address myself to all the people of this wounded continent and in particular to the youth, to you who have fought each other so much and often hated much, who at times still fight and hate each other but still recognize each other as brothers, in suffering, in humiliation, in revolt, in hope, in the sentiment that you are living a common destiny, brother through this mysterious faith that binds you to the African soil, a faith that transmits itself from generation to generation and which even exile cannot erase.

I have not come, youth of Africa, to lament with you the misfortunes of Africa. Because, Africa has no need of my laments. I have not come, youth of Africa, to take pity on your fate, because your fate is first of all in your hands. What would you do, proud youth of Africa, with my pity?

I have not come to erase the past because the past cannot be erased.

I have not come to deny mistakes or crimes — mistakes were made and crimes committed. (...)

I have come to propose to you to look together, as Africans and as French, beyond this pain and this suffering.

I have come to propose to you, youth of Africa not to forget this pain and this suffering that cannot be forgotten, but to move beyond it.

I have come to propose to you, youth of Africa, not to dwell on the past, but for us to draw together lessons from it in order to face the future together.

The tragedy of Africa is that the African has not fully entered into history. The African peasant, (...) only knew the eternal renewal of time, rhythmed by the endless repetition of the same gestures and the same words. In this imaginary world where everything starts over and over again there is no place for human adventure or for the idea of progress. In this universe where nature commands all, man escapes from the anguish of history that torments modern man, but he rests immobile in the centre of a static order where everything seems to have been written beforehand. This man (the traditional African) never launched himself towards the future. The idea never came to him to get out of this repetition and to invent his own destiny. The problem of Africa, and allow a friend of Africa to say it, is to be found here. Africa's challenge is to enter to a greater extent into history. To take from it the energy, the force, the desire, the willingness to listen and to espouse its own history. Africa's problem is to stop always repeating, always mulling over, to liberate itself from the myth of the eternal return (...) because Africa has the right to happiness like all the other continents of the world. (...) I thank you"[62].

He does not maybe recognise himself in the past actors and that is why the misfortune of Africa do not concern him. This discourse made some imminent Africans to react: Elikia M'Bokolo is one

---

62. The Speech of President Sarkozy in Dakar on July 26, 2007. (Translation by the author)

of those who do not accept the discourse of the former French president that he describe as well crafted injurious words. He writes:

"Who are these 'friends of Africa' who seem to have pleasure only in saying evil about her? Yesterday again, these people manifested enough prudence or decency- can one ever know? To be at distance from the continent when they utter unjust speeches on Africa and her people. Today their audacity has passed all terminals: it is on the very soil of Africa and in the face of Africans that they come holding out like trophies injurious words carefully crafted on the black continent"[63].

When M'Bokolo spoke of the prudence of the past he was referring to Victor Hugo, a reputed person who also said he was a friend of black people, whom Sarkozy should have quoted, he who gave a speech underscoring that he would take away from Africa any possibility of having a history:

Which land is this Africa! Asia has its own history, America has its own history, Australia itself has its own history which date to the beginning of human memory; Africa has no history, a sort of legend vast and obscure covers her (...) Africa is important to the world; such suppression of movement and circulation obstructs the world and the forward march of humanity cannot accommodate any longer that the 5th of the globe should be paralysed (...) This angry Africa has only two aspects: people, it is barbaric, desert, its savagery but it eludes more (...). In the 19th century the white man has made the black man a human, in the 20th century Europe will make of Africa a world (...) Go, people! Take over this land, Take it! To whom does it belong? No one. Take this land from God. God gives the land to men. God gave Africa to Europe. Take her[64].

---

63. M'BOKOLO Elikia, « Ce que sont ces étranges amis de l'Afrique », in *Petit Précis de remise à niveau sur l'histoire africaine a l'usage du président Sarkozy*, Paris, La Découverte, 2008, p. 9.
64. The speech of Victor Hugo pronounced at the commemorative banquet given in Paris on May 18, 1879 during the 31st anniversary of the abolition of slave trade. Notes were taken by Gaston Gerville-Réache, Brière, Paris, 1879, p. 8.

This discourse comes from a colonial ethnology which pretends bringing culture and civilisation to those who do not have one. Man has rendered historic all the elements that he has touched. There is in Africa an incommensurable culture and historical patrimony that the rest of the world must not wipe away with the wave of the hand. Cultural diversity is a non-negligible fact of human history.

What a thematic resemblance with the inacceptable 'Dakar Discourses'. All that it gives me to say loud is that the struggle against 'afro pessimism' has just started. That Africa will rise with her scars that no one doubts it; that it will craft a future for herself is something perfectly audible and will be the main subject of our analysis in the second part of this work. But Africa needs the excuses of the present and certainly not pity. That all the nations which brought this misery upon us should excuse themselves. Before any compensation they have to present their excuses.

The speech of Sarkozy contains one truth however; to open Africa to modern values, to the technological and scientific aspirations, in short to development. But if the African has not entered enough into history as the president has said, if the peasants or the country folk in Africa since the beginning stay put on the same practices and changing of the seasons, this problem is not only anthropological. It is not also linked with the African traditions and customs (the president pretends to know more and forget that out traditions and customs also have values). The conspiracy and the exclusion of which Africa is always an object also has a role to play. Africa is excluded from the major decisions. The IMF and the World Bank imposed structural adjustment measures which only increased austerity and poverty. The young African, even the most ambitious are not exposed to value education. Quality laboratories are not available and the experts leaving. At the Berlin Conference was partitioned disoriented and crumble. We would need another Berlin conference to open for her true perspectives of progress. The history of the colonisers is not the only one to be heard, Mr President. The peoples are different but equal and that, it is good that all humanity hears it if we do not want to create differences between the colonisers and the colonised.

On July 27th, 2007 president Sarkozy was on a visit to Gabon and there he affirmed that everything cannot be put on the back of colonisation in order to justify the deplorable state of Africa. In Africa, there are unacceptable and autocratic regimes here and there. Corruption, genocide, dictatorships do not result from colonisation. Africans have their part of the responsibility in the present tragedy of the continent but the president cannot wipe everything by just waving the hand the part of colonisation in the present evil of which has befallen Africa.

Our dictators were all good students or puppets at the service of the colonisers. To my knowledge, Rwanda still insists on the fact that France participated in the 1992 genocide. The fact that Africa is partly responsible for her woes should not make others to forget the part of the responsibility of the colonising powers.

We can accuse what we can in the African traditions and some aspects of her culture, and agricultural methods. But one cannot come to Africa to exonerate colonisation and refuse to make excuses. To endure and to swallow such words is not acceptable for us. On the other hand, to admit this fault can create for us, the descendants of the colonised, some space of humanity and development perspectives to revitalise Africa.

Africa does not have history because she has been excluded from the history of humanity. By the slave trade and colonisation the card of poverty, of misery of Africa came to be. We would like to have excuses to diffuse the trauma of the continent. Today, our hands are no more tied and our legs in chains like the times of the slave trade and colonisation, but the black conscience is still a victim of this heavy past. Today, a greater part of African do not value all that is African in order to privilege what comes from the West. There, is one of the scars of the past that a just repentance will deliver us from. We cannot just easily ignore this drama:

"Colonialism is far from being a golden rocket. Giant statue in front of which, frightened or fascinated multitudes came to prostrate, he concealed in reality a huge hollow. Metal carcass output splendid jewels, he participated also the Beast and manure. Slow blaze dispersing around its plumes of smoke, it sought to establish itself both as ritual and as an event; as speech, gesture and wisdom, story/tale and myth, like murder and accident. And it is partly because of its formidable ability of proliferation and metamorphosis that made trembles the presence of those whom he had enslaved, seeping into their dreams, filling them with the most frightful nightmares, before snatching their atrocious lamentation. Colonization meanwhile, was not a technology or a simple device. It was only ambiguities. It was also a complex, scaffolding of certainties, some more illusory than others: the power of the false (the power of lies)[65].

Colonisation was a powerful lie which became victorious without reason. To bandage a deep wound like that of the slave trade and colonisation all the limits have to be shaken. Repentance for me is a necessary evil which could give back confidence to the African and to re-establish the just links with the West.

My country Congo called 'Democratic' is full of extraordinary natural resources and her land and underground are very rich. This country remains poor for decades now. Corruption, dictatorship, wars; these are the reasons often advanced. Faced with this geological scandal where poverty has chosen to reside in this country more envied in the world, I will avoid mentioning the responsibility of the Belgian king Leopold II who after the 1884 conference of Berlin, has made this country his private property: the land, the underground, inhabitants and all that was found in this country belonged to him by right. This king cut off at will, the hands of my ancestors and

---

65. MBEMBE Achille, *Sortir de la grande nuit: Essai sur l'Afrique colonisée*, Paris, La Découverte, 2010-2013, p. 1.

plundered our riches. Tell me if this treatment does not contribute to our maintaining in misery and frustration; tell me if it is not yet time that they present their excuses to us!

I.4. Africa in the post colonial society

> *The political attributions cannot be conceived without responsibility; and the political responsibility of the leaders of the people is not conceivable so long as the people itself is not in the state of looking at least at the main lines, the conduct of politics. The weak attitudes of the people, taking it in all its totality, are still very far from responding, in the way in which since 1926, the political competences have left for India[66].*

The meaning of the responsibility, that is what must characterise the political attributions. That is the view of the Bishop's Conference of Congo in 1998 of the socio-political crisis that affected the country between 1956 and 1998:

> *The socio-political crisis that touches our country affects the people in its whole. But it is above all a crisis of the political class/elite. As you can understand, there is nothing worst for a people than to be led by leaders in crisis. That is why we make an urgent appeal to all the political class of Zaire so that it will free itself from the vices which it has erected as an ideal and as a project of the society. According to African tradition, the leader is a model. The progress in our country and elsewhere, depend of the high moral and civic virtues of the leaders; their conversion and change of power, conditions peace and the good of the people. In the same line, leaders worthy of this name do not conclude favourable economic investment contracts in the interest of the nation[67].*

---

66. VAN WING , *Etudes Bakongo II. Religion et magie. Mémoire*, Institut Royal Belge, p. 81.
67. *Conférence Episcopale du Congo, Le discours sociopolitique de l'Eglise catholique du Congo (1956-1998) Eglise et Société*, Tome 1, Textes rassemblées et présentées par Léon de Saint Moulin, Facultés Catholiques de Kinshasa, 1998, p. 439.

We cannot talk of the post-colonial society of Africa without asking the political responsibility of their leaders and those of the people itself. The slave trade is far beyond us, the colonisation has ended since half century for many African countries. And apart from some quiet improvement here and there, our post colonial society cannot hide its apparent failures. It seems today absurd to continue to accuse the past without Africa putting itself in question. The political responsibility of our leaders and those of the people is no doubt in my view. This is what we are going to bring out and discuss briefly.

1.4.1. The political responsibility of African leaders

I do not know really if African leaders are conscious of the weight of our history, the one which does not leave any possibility to make worse what is already deplorable. The binding misery, the economic stagnation and above all the authoritarianism in the exercise of power show that we do not give a good image of Africa. In doing so, we show that there is a growing gap dividing African countries between them with two emergent countries (South Africa and Nigeria), developing countries and stagnating and regressing countries. We indicate here the political responsibility of African leader described by Achille Mbembe who wants to show in his book « *Afriques indociles* » or *"Rebellious Africa"* that:

> *"The post colonial powers can no longer pretend any legitimacy in governing continually with exceptional measures. I understand that the challenge of today is to make the African political systems ready to make use of the fundamental freedom of the indigenous people as an asset, a resource to serve the objectives they proclaim. I emphasised the fact that in the last years, they revitalised areas of disorder, nourished causes of injustice and revolts, and so offering to external powers the excuse to limit the margin of autonomy of an already poor local societies. It comes out that instead of favouring the way of creating riches and reduce the pains of the indigenous, the authoritarian principle proved, in the specific case of the black continent, to have stop the above. This obstacle is rendered dramatic by the fact that two factors which*

are, on the one hand, the powerful ascension of the society and the ingenuity to resist the hegemonic pretentions of the postcolonial state; and on the other hand the general context of scarcity and shortage made worse by the international constraints, reducing the manoeuvre of African governments and poses in critical terms, the problem of sharing power and riches[68].

The view of Achille Mbembe seems to have reflected the actual state of governance of the continent by some leaders: little efforts in the creation of wealth and employment and always more shrewdness in strengthening their authoritarian power. Barak Obama, the president of the United States of America, during his first official visit as president, gave an important speech for the emancipation of the African continent, on the 11th of July 2009 in Ghana. His optimistic comments were inviting African leaders to take over the political and economic reins, in order to bring out the continent from the repeated crises. We must start with this simple proposal, Obama said in Accra:

"The future of Africa belongs to African themselves", prosecutor who Africa "is not away from the business of the world" and need for strong men does not have, but of solid institutions[69].

This speech seems to be fallen on the ears. We are in 2014 and several African presidents, inter alia those of Burkina Faso, of Burundi and both Congos, are thinking of making constitutional changes to the limitation of mandate so as to present themselves. Power sharing is a true bone of contention. These small constitutional arrangements undermine change of government. Here is a list of leaders who came to power either following a coup d'état, or because fraudulent elections termed democratic, and who maintained themselves in power for than 20 years: Teodoro Obiang Nguema Mbasogo of Equatorial Guinea, 35 years in power since August 3rd,

68. MBEMBE Achille, *Afriques indociles. Christianisme, pouvoir et Etat en société postcoloniale*, Paris, Karthala, 1988, p. 154.
69. The Speech of President Barak Obama on 11th July 2009 in Accra, Ghana.

1979; José Edouardo Dos Santos of Angola, 35 years in power since September 10th, 1979; Paul Biya of Cameroon, 34 years in power since November 6th, 1982; Yoweri Museveni of Uganda, 30 years in power since January 29th 1986; Robert Mugabe of Zimbabwe, 29 years with the power since December 31st 1987 (He is oldest Head of State in Africa still in power); Idriss Deby Itno of Chad, 26 years in power since December 2nd, 1990; Blaise Compaoré of Burkina Faso, 27 years in power since October 15th, 1987 (He has just been driven out by a popular uprising); Omar El-Béchir of Sudan, 28 years in power since 1989; Issayas Afeworki of Eritrea, 23 years in power since May 1993, a regime without neither presidential election nor freedom of the press.

These power hungry men have predecessors who died in power in this postcolonial Africa: Félix Houphouet Boigny of the Cote d'Ivoire remained in power since independence of his country until his death in 1993 at the 88 years age; Desiré Joseph Mobutu Sese Kuku Ngbendu Waza Banga of Zaire in power from 1965 to 1997, Gnassingbé Eyadéma of Togo in power from 1967 until his death in 2005, El Hadj Omar Bongo Ondimba of Gabon in power from 1967 until his death in 2009, making 42 year-long reign. The two last had as successors their own children.

How can solid institutions be set up if certain leaders believe themselves indispensable? How can wealth be created if these men, who are among the richest of the continent, deposit half of their fortune abroad? The actual state of the post postcolonial society in general is a non accidental failure, but rather orchestrated by an irresponsible ruling class living at the expense of lower classes which struggle from day to day to survive despite everything. Africa is at the top being the continent with less services and infrastructures.

1.4.2. The responsibility of the people

The people of Africa have reached the height of their difficult describable endurance. It is the feeling of not counting on anybody to improve their situation. A continent abandoned to her own initiative and/or to international assistance. The responsibility of the people lies in the fact that they have not reacted; they let things be done to and for them. The various aspects of the African tragedy must be examined in the light of a total awakening. The current trend is rather that of the exile and the escape failing to have ahead been able to clear us a specific way to our needs and our rhythm. If nothing is done to reverse this curve, then the complex of inferiority, kneeling and despair will not leave us as soon as. The escape of youth by the clandestine immigration and that of the brains is a disavowal of the continent by its living strength which takes the bet to go to seek a better life in Occident.

It is true that the working conditions are difficult; there is a real deficit out of equipment in the laboratories and libraries. For those which have a job, the wages are too low to allow an adequate standard of living. The escape of the young people and that of the brains is not the cause, but the consequence of some of something: political frustrations, especially the difficulty which African has compared to the expression of the rights in their own countries. The clandestine immigration and the brain drain, even if they can seem beneficial for those which leave have a negative impact on the development and constitute a loss for the whole of the company. The abandonment of the African ship between the hands of the unconscious captains who lead it to the shipwreck, here is the responsibility for those which leave. Failing to fight to change Africa of the inside, they choose to change world. Let us not be so pessimistic only that. All those which leave always do not have the happiness which they search. Any departure should not either be associated with an escape, mobility is a total question. Our speech should not be seen like suicidal. The purpose of it is to return each one to its own conscience. Africa needs not to be continuously shed tears/ whimper on its past, but to clearly identify to take the true turn towards political revolutions and the social jolts which put the interest of the people at the heart of any vision of the world. We have spoken about our miseries it is time that we approach and take on embark what seems to be for us ways of hope.

II – Our Hopes

Nobody can develop Africa better than ourselves. With these lines, we would like to dream of Africa as we would have wished that she is, as she would have been notwithstanding vicissitudes of her history.

II.1. The fight against the putting of the individual under supervision to the benefit of the group.

A challenge to overcome is to make a scientific means of production a priority. To arrive at it, formation is really the best investment and nevertheless our developing African society puts the individual under the supervision of the taboos and a too heavy traditional hierarchy. This kind of system does not allow the individual to affirm his/her dignity and neither chats freely the course of his/her destiny. There is a tension between the need to advance towards more autonomy and the ever strong place that heteronomy has in the mentalities of people.

As we shall be seeing it in the next point, in the history of transposing ourselves into the world of others, one of the great inventions of the Enlightenment period in the West, is to have given to the individual his/her place in society. On this point, Africa has a lot to do. The cultural obstacles to overcome are huge but not impossible. The question here is to know how to realise a deep social transformation and a true improvement in the level of live on the Western model when we know, and we agree with Barthelemy Adoukounou, that an individual does not exist except in relation to the group:

"In the African conception of human being, the human person is a inalie-
nable property of the group, that is why the dead must return on the earth
where the umbilical cord was buried; the place of birth must be also the place
where we disappear to the "land of life"[70].

In keeping our traditional values like those of solidarity and the respect of the elderly, it seems evident to us to deny all other social behaviours which block the blossoming of reason and the human personality and which block the individual to expose himself to new realities. We would not like to become spokespersons of the deconstruction of communitarianism, but to make through this text, a plea for an education that would take into account individualism within the meaning that promotes each individual who is at the same time an autonomous and a relational subject. This education should return to the compliance with the rules necessary for individual and collective work. This education should aim at the respect and the reinforcement of the rights and fundamental freedoms of each individual. This presupposes the establishment of norms to be applied and respected by all. For Alain Touraine, the reconstruction of personal identity does not pass by the identifying with a global order, but by the recognition of each individual.

"The new cultural movements refuse any identification with a social category;
they call on the subject himself, on his dignity or his self esteem like force of
combination of instrumental roles and of individuality. That which supposes
the recognition of the psychological and cultural specificity of each one and of
his capacity of creation, founded on the reason or on an assertion even more
direct from creativity."[71]

---

70. ADOUKONOU Barthelemy, *Jalons pour une théologie africaine. Essai d'une herméneutique chrétienne du Vodun dahoméen*, Tome II : Etude ethnologique, Paris Editions Lethielleux, Namur culture et vérité, 1980, p. 44.
71. TOURAINE Alain, *Pourrons-nous vivre ensemble ? Egaux et différents*, Paris, Fayard, 1997, p. 135.

We aim at a reorganization of the social order which is primarily marked by injustices, marginalisation and alienations in this society where the individual is oppressed and/or where discomfort and the lethargy is nothing but spreading. We would like to rise against a form of status quo which does not say its name: since the ancestors one always proceeded thus, one should not revolutionize our manners. Let us keep what frees us but let us also evolve certain aspects of our life which ever since gave us rather disappointing results. Let us look on the side of education and dare to put the individual at the centre. It is always the community which determines the place of the individual, let us try to make it possible for this individual to establish himself/herself by personal and considered choice, his/her place in the community.

II. 2. To Challenge ourselves like the Age of Enlightenments in the West.

The imagination of Africa faces various challenges. These include the accused behind the continent in relation to the use of information technology (emerging culture), the proliferation of sects, poverty, political instability, social disorientation and many others. One of the often overlooked challenges, but that seems relevant to discuss here is the erasure of the subject. In many situations the individual lives in anonymity, lost in the spring clannish community, tribal or ethnic. How to continue the development effort when one is faced with such challenges? Given this negative panorama for optimism and assert forcefully that these difficulties are surmountable?

To meet these challenges, it seems important to question ourselves, to change the face of our anthropology and to make humanity new. This challenge will perhaps upset our sociological field and reorient the conduct of our future actions.

It is the extent which we are capable of challenging our traditional anthropology by placing the human subject in the centre and empowering him/her in the face of his/her acts that our revolution and endeavour will become effective. Putting people at the centre is not to be confused with the loss of our community values such as self-help and others, it is simply to query reason, the good sense of each one and allow him/her to speak. These are some ways inherited from the Enlightenments that we intend to explore to enable Africa to also develop a school of thought.

An Africa that would make School

It is often with desolation that we notice the absence of the African contribution in several areas within the group of nations. Africa should assert its identity, and that she brings something more to others. "No one is so poor as to have nothing to give, no one is so rich as to receive nothing, a popular proverb says." All fields of science require not only a thorough research, but also production. We need classical thinkers who would be points of reference for the rest of humanity. Since the pre-Socratic times, through the centuries of the Enlightenments, the West has always produced thinkers who threw light on human reflection. Socrates, Aristotle, Plato, Thomas Aquinas, Kant, Einstein, Newton, Descartes, Paul Ricoeur, Karl Rahner, to name but a few; they continue to exercise their influence on scientific debates and conferences.

Africa still lags behind in creating a true school of thought. Throwing an eye on what is being done elsewhere can inspire us. Without pretending to reproduce comprehensively the legacy of the Enlightenments, we would like to briefly point out a period/epoch/time, which in its merits, but also in its heydays has revolutionized the way of life and thinking in the West. If the Catholic Church in Africa claims its specificity in the representation of the same faith in God as the rest of the world for example, it is useful that African theologians are striving to bring out the plausibility and the peculiarities of this out[72].

---

72. We recognise here the immense work of the African heralds in this field. :

II.2.1 The merit of the Age of Enlightenments

History could well direct us. We will take the time of the Enlightenments for model which established, according to us, the individual in his rights and his dignity. This system is fascinating because it found the right balance between individualism and the communal. It produced great thinkers like Emmanuel Kant. Without going into details, we want to partly assume the heritage of this person which especially consists in releasing the people of the barriers of ignorance. The time of Enlightenment marks in a considerable way, the starting point of the development of the Occident.

Instead of giving credit to superstition and encouraging ignorance and dependence, the Enlightenments believe in the capacity to change the world by the reason. It is the century of the emancipation of the human spirit and body. Kant is incontestably the philosopher who gave a true answer to our search for direction in the Enlightenments through the formation that we mention here below:

"The Enlightenment is man's emergence from his self-imposed (infancy) nonage. Nonage is the inability to use one's own understanding without another's guidance. This nonage is self-imposed if its cause lies not in lack of understanding but in indecision and lack of courage to use one's own mind without another's guidance. Dare to know! Sapere aude! 'Have the courage to use your own understanding,' is therefore the motto of the enlightenment"[73].

ELA Jean-Marc, *Le cri de l'homme Africain. Questions aux Chrétien et aux Eglises d'Afrique*, Paris, L'Harmattan, 1993 p. From the same author: *Ma foi d'Africain*, Paris, Karthala, 1985, 224p. "La relève missionnaire en Afrique", dans B.T.A., vol. 7, No. 1314, Janvier-décembre, 1985. Read also ADOUKONOU Barthelemy, *Jalons pour une théologie africaine. Essai d'une herméneutique chrétienne du Vodun dahomeen*, Tome II, Paris Les Editions Lethielleux, Namur, culture et vérité, 1980. See SANTEDI KINKUPU Leonard, *Les défis de l'Evangélisation dans l'Afrique contemporaine*, Paris, Editions Karthala, 2005. From the same author : *La mission du prêtre dans l'œuvre de la promotion humaine*, Kinshasa, Editions du Seminaire Jean XXIII, 1995 ; *Dogme et inculturation en Afrique. Perspective d'une théologie de l'invention*, Paris, Karthala, 2003, 203 p.

73. KANT Immanuel, *Réponse a la question: Qu'est-ce que les lumières?*, translated by

A critical subject is introduced into a civilisation where the legal universe and the dictates of duty are essential to him. The conception of his relationship with the world passes by the respect of the law. In such an approach, personal initiative is encouraged but remains all the same structured by the law which is supposed to guarantee the coexistence through the respect of the freedom and the dignity of each one.

To direct action in the good sense, i.e. that of the good, Kant would say that nature supplemented the will by reason. Reason guides human acts. She is the one who discerns what is necessary to be done or not, which gives oneself credibility of action, the maxims, according to the laws which the subject recognises as good and just. His action has a moral value, if he obeys the law, and if he accomplishes it, he acts by duty. A duty is an action which respects the law. Morality is an action by duty, but by a duty freely assumed. For that, it is necessary that the human will is directed by reason.

Human Reason obtains at the age of Enlightenment, a simply autonomous status. We realise some in the Enlightenments philosophy of Ernest Cassirer, quoted by Michael Foessel:

"Reason' is the meeting point and the centre of expansion of the century, the expression of all her desires, all her efforts, her wants and of her achievements"[74].

The Enlightenments affirm that the obstacles should be fought so that man can live and fulfil himself/herself fully. Ignorance, superstition and intolerance are obstacles that only a man enlightened by reason can rise up to.

Jean Mondot, Presses Univesitaires de Bordeaux,2007,p.79.
74. FOESSEL Michael, "Refaire les Lumières?", in *Esprit*, No. 357, Aout-Septembre 2009, p. 151-160.

II.2.2 Paradoxes of the Age of Enlightenments

We are fascinated by the Enlightenments, but we do not adhere without reserve to its imperialism making of reason the only credo of the human being. We express doubts about the fact that some of the thinkers of Enlightenments reduce all the desires and all the aspirations of man to only the will and power of reason. This is a form of limitation of freedom and a sort contradiction in regard to the very aim of the Enlightenments.

To bring everything back to reason is a dangerous radicalisation and besides, the controversies are not late in coming. Even if we adhere to the important place that the Enlightenments grant to autonomy and the individual subject, we can conceal its harmful aspects that we challenge and contest. We admit in Kant to have had the merit to propose to man a noble way capable of drawing him out of the state of nonage or infancy to which he has deliberately let himself go into, that of rationality. Nevertheless we do not understand that he can support in a fundamental way the total inclination of man to only reason. On the moral level this position appears unacceptable to us. To obey only reason can result in making of a good par excellence whereas we know how much reason is sometimes limited, therefore capable of mistake and induce into error and evil.

> *"The Enlightenments are fatal by themselves because, applicant that only what underwent the examination of the reason the right has to remain, they are reduced to the criticism of the prejudices, which however are constitutive of the human spirit »*[75]

To reduce man to his only rationality is a form of exclusive fundamentalism which is used only for the reduction of any individual freedom that the Enlightenments promoted everywhere.

It seems useful to evoke, in illustrating our case, the type of conflict relationship which existed on the one hand between the

---

75. BRAHIMI Frédéric, "L'empire divin des préjugés. Joseph de Maistre contre l'esprit éclairé", in *Esprit*, No. 357, Aout-Septembre 2009, pp. 136-149

Enlightenments and on the other hand monotheisms. The interest will be put here on the controversy of Enlightenments/Christianity.

"The relation between the Enlightenments and the monotheisms is polemical, in spite of the nuances according to the national traditions and confessions"[76].

A disagreement between the Enlightenments and religions was born around the opposition faith/reason. The Enlightenments wanted to put an end to the influence of clericalism on reason. They sought to release man from a certain kind of religious totalitarian which put reason under (*tutelle*) supervision/guardianship. So that the religions cannot impose in fact their hegemony on the faithful, even on the State itself, the Enlightenments sometimes went as far as preaching the exclusion of the theologian. The field of the belief underwent a total rupture. Has the radical position of the Enlightenments consisted in making tabula rasa of the influence of religion in order, starting from a new spirit and new methods, to rebuild the concept of God?

"At the roots of the Enlightenments and modernity, there are thus a deep claim of freedom of conscience and a true war of liberation against a theologico-political domination some of whose thinkers, the most radical of them, will draw all the consequences of historical and mental rupture in the fields of metaphysics, of ethics, of religion and of politics"[77].

The Enlightenments move away from the "blind" belief in God and it want simply to impose the main line of thought according to which the expression of all human desires passes through the reason. The human spirit conceives nothing better than what it generates by its own means. In the faith/reason, the Enlightenments try to eliminate the superstition and the irrational in religious belief. One

76. SCHEGEL Jean-Louis, "Les religions avec, après ou contre les Lumières", in *Esprit*, No. 357, Aout-Septembre 2009, pp. 189-212.
77. BOVE Laurent, "Lumières 'radicales' ou 'modérées' : une lecture à partir de Spinoza », in *Esprit*, No. 357, Aout-Septembre 2009, pp. 125-135.

can find an advantage and a disadvantage in this radicalisation of faith.

Advantage of the reduction of faith to reason

The force of such an approach lies in the fact that the faithful has solid arguments that can be used to justify his/her faith, he/she is not easily deceived and manipulated neither by the clergy nor religion. One believes by conviction and can justify rationally and without naivety the reason of his/her faith. On this religious question of the statute of belief, Jean-Marc Ferry supports the idea that the spirit of the Enlightenments is modelled on the dialogue faith and reason, a dialogue which he finds beneficial to religion itself:

"One can see an advantage for religion itself because of the longings that profane requests for explanation constitute. That obliges the religions to test for themselves their own convictions… On entering onto the public space, the speech of the clergy is subjected to the common imperfect/fallible discipline. She breaks with the style of complicity to face the requirements of criticism. If it is true that our public political spaces have need now of religious enlightenments, it is, reciprocally by interiorising the critical dimension that religion could recharge its capital of experience and reactivate its hermeneutical potential"[78].

The faith needs conviction. The believer should not lose his critical spirit to follow blindly any form of supposedly revealed religion. By the requirement of criticism, the Enlightenments introduced a profound change, that of breaking free from ignorance and superstition. To believe, it is necessary to have conviction and deep reasons.

While remaining opposed to the Enlightenments, of which Timothy Radcliffe, an English Dominican priest, points out some deviations, inter alia its alienating categories (Cartesian individualism) and its culture of control, he however does not reject in block the

78. FERRY Jean-Marc, « Lumières 'radicales' ou 'modérées' : une lecture à partir de Spinoza », in *Esprit*, No. 357, Aout-Septembre 2009, pp. 161-169.

heritage of the Enlightenments. For him, the Church should be inspired by it so as to call herself into question, to be renewed and to enter into a vital interaction with the world which surrounds her. Instead of being a culture of control, the Church should be an oasis of freedom of Christ:

> *"If the Church wants to develop an elaborate healthy relation with society, without cutting off herself in a ghetto nor to lose itself in the limbos of assimilation, then we need a dynamic catholic culture. That is to say universities and faculties in which we can, in confidence to explore our faith, to ask difficult questions, to test new ideas, to play with these ideas… I expect a massive revival of the religious life very soon, including in the West"[79].*

The Enlightenments has been at the start of the emergence of a new world. It was a period extremely beneficial in the history of humanity. Man knows henceforth that to question oneself is not only an obviousness, but also a need. It is a need for Africa.

Limits of the reduction of faith to reason

Of which reason does the Enlightenment speak? Can one exclude God the master and the creator of everything from human reason? Can reason explain everything? The inherent danger in the reduction of faith to the reason by the Enlightenments is, wanting to remove God (the inspirer of all rationality) and to speak only about the human character from reason. The rational justification, the Cartesian model is neither the only one capable of explaining all phenomena in nature nor all the situations of human life:

> *"The Enlightenments, indeed, is not only confidence with regard to the achievements of reason, it is first of all, the consciousness of the human character of this reason. The privilege granted to the analysis, the refusal (common to Newton and Voltaire) of the unverifiable assumptions, the primacy of experimentation and the abandonment of the hope to raise the "veil of Isis"*

79. RADCLIFFE Timothy, o.p, «Quelle forme pour l'Eglise de demain?» , in *La Documentation Catholique*, N°2432, du 18/10/2009.

which hides the essence of things: as many characteristics which mark the affinity of the Enlightenments with the concept of finitude'[80].

The exclusion of God and fixing on man and his reason are elements of the mentality of Enlightenments of which we must liberate ourselves. The faith of the believer cannot rest only on logical and rigorous deductions of reason. It takes support on the total abandonment and confidence which one has in God. The road towards the unknown is part of faith. We passed by this long turn through the Enlightenments to find the place of autonomy in the life of man.

In present society where knowledge becomes increasingly more specialised and of sectors, it appears even more necessary that African decision makers should invest in the human being with the aim of offering an invaluable contribution to the aspirations of our society. We live in an era of deep and rapid changes. A specific vision of the African universe is essential with all urgency so as to give back hope to the people submerged in the mud of misery.

II.3 The deconstruction of the unilateral speech on development

It is a question of working with a true transmission of power between the decision makers and development project engineers and the recipients who are the poor of the Third World countries in general and those of Africa in particular. The implication, which is the participation of the recipients, is an essential key to the development of the African continent.

We tackle the question of the participation in the approaches of development in the countries of the South as a reason for hope. This question is really central because it puts in perspective the needs for the targeted populations, the actors and the various development projects.

---

80. FOESSEL Michael, *Op. Cit.*, pp. 151-160.

Participation is truly a key concept, because nobody can develop given cultural setting/milieu better than the population concerned. It is an alternative approach of the culture which calls for collaboration, self esteem, the owning of projects and confidence. We note here that the lack of participation was the cause of the failure in many development projects conceived in high place, i.e. by the experts who do not take into account the contingencies on the ground.

The questions we are concerned about are to highlight (on all levels), the degree of participation between the various actors from the design to the realization and the evaluation of a development project. Who are the actors who come into play in such a chain? We feel the need to have a small historical framework in order to point out clearly some keywords and to situate our work.

In the 1990s, in the countries of the South, the pressure of the civil society is felt and allows the acceptance of the humanitarian norms (Mary Kaldor, *Global Civil Society*, 2003: 132). Famine and hunger, diseases and the loss of the human lives, extreme poverty is the battle ahead of us and history (the Preface of Bono of the book of Sachs, *The end of poverty*, 2004, XV). It is the decade during which many struggles and fights for social justice give way to a social policy that states must carry out, that which deals with the needs of the people, especially the most underprivileged.

* **Poverty, civil society and international aid**

The review *The Independent* of September 10, 2003 invites decision makers to tackle the question of inequalities in the world: two billion seven hundred thousand (2.07billon) inhabitants of the six billion lives on the planet live on less than two dollars per day. Governments take from the people more than they give them.

The Millennium Agenda started in 2000 for the development and the eradication of poverty in the world has not given expected results. The set objectives aimed among other things to reducing to half, between 1990 and 2015, the number of individuals living with less than one dollar per day, reducing extreme poverty and the hunger. We note that a year after 2015 these objectives are far from being reached All the objectives which we reproduce below will still require more money and political will to be attained.

1. To eradicate extreme poverty and hunger.
2. To ensure universal primary education for all.
3. To promote gender equality and empowerment of women.
4. To reduce infant mortality
5. To improve maternal health.
6. To fight diseases
7. To ensure a sustainable human environment
8. To develop a global partnership for development.

It is necessary to change the living conditions of the people where they are instead of making of them objects of charity of the West. Extreme poverty is a regional problem with 93% of the poor of the world living in Africa and Asia. The rest is located in Latin America and Eastern Europe. Kothari and Minogue (2002) think that the concept of development would be more powerful if it revealed its own secret, i.e. what we understand by development because this term is ambiguous. It is a question of the relationship of power by a simple rhetoric with populist labels in vogue: civil society, reduction of poverty, participation. They recognize all the same that certain NGO's directed by civil society groups are active in local communities and making efforts in moving the frontiers.

*Civil society and NGOs between 1990 and 2000

Civil society and NGOs initially, concentrated in the beginning on charity activities in the countries of the South. Secondly, they directed their activities towards development. Thirdly, they took on the role of catalyst so that the people become the centre of the development on the local level. Fourthly, global civil society aligned itself with new social movements for example the environmentalists, human rights and feminists movements (Korten, 1997).

Our key words will thus be: participation, development project, poverty and the actors. At the heart of our work, our objective is to find the centre of redistribution even of the transfer of power between the hands of the projects engineers towards those of the recipients.

Our methodology will consist with an analysis of texts in order to be able to diagonally approach the challenges and practices of development to be put forward for the countries of the South.

- Jean-Pierre Olivier de Sardan, "Les trois approche en anthropologie du développent", *Tiers Monde*, 2001, Tome 42, n°168, pp.729-754.

- Leroy MAYA (2005), *Méthodes participatives dans le cadre des rapports nord-sud. Une revue critique de la littérature*

- Marilou MATHIEU, "Ballade d'un expert anthropologue sur les traces de la MARP", in *Les enquêtes participatives en débat. Ambition, pratiques et enjeu*, Paris, Gret, Karthala, Icra, 2000.

- Stéphane de Tapia, *Systee migratoire euro-méditerranéen. Effets des transferts financiers dans les pays d'origine*, Strasbourg, Edition du Conseil de l'Europe

- Sylvie BRUNEL, *L'Afrique*, Rosny-sous-Bois, Éditions Bréal, 2004, 239p.

We shall take as plan the three approaches suggested by Jean Pierre Olivier de Sardan that we will analyse in parallel with other texts: 1. Another discourse on development, 2. The populist approach, 3. Tangle of social logics and the heterogeneity of the actors.

*Another discourse on development

The question of development must be treated as objectively possible. What makes development? Should there be economic choices with the disastrous consequences for the people? These choices were often made by foreign experts without direct link with the population concerned. The gap is often very large between the speech of the developers and the social practices on the ground. The expert must play the part of facilitator, that which helps so that the project succeeds. He should not be the only decision maker.

Jean Pierre Olivier de Sardan starts from an anthropological perspective which supposes the clarification of the concept of development. This one cannot be ebbed out without taking into account all the forms of interactions and all the complexity of the social practices which go with them. He conceives development in close link with anthropology:

"Development is not indeed for us anything else except the whole of actions of all kinds which are claimed of it, from near or by far (on the side of the "developers" as those of the "developed"), in the diversity of their acceptances, significances and practices. The existence of a "developmental configuration" the complex whole of institutions, of flux and of actors, for whom development constitutes a resource, a trade, a market, a challenge, or a strategy, is enough to legitimate the existence of a social anthropology which takes development like object of study or entry"[81].

This anthropological vision of development emphasises the coexistence of several factors and several actors in all practices of development. It is an approach which has the virtue to deconstruct the hegemony of the only speech of developer who comes as the saviour of the poor. For us who come from a country known as of the South, the Democratic Republic of Congo in Africa, since the independence of our countries i.e. around the years 1960 (for most of our countries) to our days, only one word returns in all the debates: "development". What does one seek exactly? The more we search the more underdevelopment progresses with very disastrous social consequences: impoverishment, massive unemployment, rise of malnutrition, the reappearance of endemic diseases which were

---

81. Jean-Pierre Olivier de Sardan, « Les trois approches en anthropologie du développement », in *Tiers-Monde*, 2001, Tome 42, No. 168, p. 731.

believed suppressed: tripanosomiasis, typhoid fever, cholera and all opportunist diseases associated with AIDS.

We speak about development since more than half a century, but African societies continue to oscillate between resourcefulness and the idea of every man for himself. What do we seek that development did allow finding? To develop it is necessary at all costs to boost the responsibility of the recipients, the auto-appropriation of the concept of development. The eye of the anthropologist is to identify what is being sought:

"The anthropologist must often risk being in conflict with others in order to reach varied information allowing him to put into perspective an accurate information"[82].

In Africa just like in other countries of the South, there should be taking into account of the social and cultural dimensions before speaking about development. The complexity of the concept is translated even in the actions which the emigrants try to undertake with their countries of origin. Relying on the experts and the researchers working in the connection migration-development, professor Stéphane de Tapia affirms that:

"The development of the countries of origin of the international migration is a phenomenon highly complex, relatively easy to describe, extremely difficult to model and transfer"[83].

For Stéphane de Tapia the connection migration-development supposes a good knowledge and a better comprehension of all the systems which come into play. To develop in our estimation, must include the participation of all the actors, the recognition of the complexity of each situation, work to which anthropologists devote

82. MARILOU Mathieu, « Ballade d'un expert anthropologue sur les traces de la MARP » in *Les enquêtes participatives en débat : ambition, pratiques et enjeux*, Paris, Karthala, 2000, p. 344.

83. DE TAPIA Stéphane, *Système migratoire euro-méditerranéen. Effets de transferts financiers dans le pays d'origine*, Strasbourg, Édition du Conseil de l'Europe, p.96.

themselves better than the financial investors. Participation serves to reinforce the capacities of all the actors and to develop the consensus in the realisation of the project.

Populist approach

Populism was often confused with "deconstructionism", because its speech is unilateral, that is to say, based on the only thought of the developer excluding those to be developed. All the knowledge to be implemented is hijacked by the bureaucracy of the institutions of development. Populism also uses a fluid language on development. All is directed towards the economy, the technique and management. The knowledge of the people on the ground either is ignored, or used with an ideological or demagogic aim. They make use of the knowledge of weak in public speaking in a form of rhetoric.

"One can indeed distinguish an "ideological populism" with which it would be advisable to break (illustrated by the classical work of Chambers, 1990-1993) and a "methodological populism", necessary for the anthropological investigation. The ideological populism paints reality with the colours of its desires, and has a magic vision of the popular knowledge. The methodological populism, considers in its turn that the groups or social actors from "bottom" have knowledge and strategies which it is advisable to explore, but without coming to a conclusion about their value or their validity"[84].

The populist approach uses the popular practices not to credit to them, but to give credit to the demagogue. There is prevalence here of one discourse to the detriment of the knowledge of those to be developed.

Olivier de Sardan distinguishes the ideological populism which idealises the capacities of the people from the methodological populism which is satisfied to describe the pragmatic resources (even the most unimportant) of any actor.

---

84. Jean-Pierre Olivier de Sardan, *Op. Cit.*, p. 738.

At all the levels it is necessary to take into account the scientific knowledge of the experts who tend to predict everything, the local knowledge which has the merit to be practical and informal even if it were not recognized yet as scientific, the field of development being that in which there is inevitably the impossibility all of predicting everything. Not to combine scientific knowledge with the practical local knowledge led many projects to failure:

> *"It is because the great centralised and planned schemes of social transformation (urban, revolutionary, developpemental) do not take it into account that they always fail"*[85].

It is perhaps on the side of the combination of the global and the local that should be sought the key of success of development projects. There is a great need for participation and it would become effective if it led to the realisation of projects which start from below and the role of the experts being that of catalysts. It is within this framework that the authors as Maya Leroy will privilege a method as the MARP (Accelerated Method of Participative Research):

> *"Most known of the participative methods of the ground is the MARP (Accelerated Method of participative Research). It is a question of carrying out fast diagnoses on the ground, with the local populations. The populations here are the "experts" in the system and strongly take part in the development of the objectives of the project"*[86].

The process of participation is difficult to be set up. It is confronted with several factors: time, money… but it is the interface by which one arrives at building a minimum of common objectives. The recipients have to take part in the execution as well as in the evaluation of the project.

---

85. Jean-Pierre Olivier de Sardan, *Op. Cit.*, p. 740.
86. MAYA Leroy, *L'analyse stratégique de la gestion environnementale : un cadre théorique pour penser l'efficacité en matières d'environnent*, 2005/2 (vol. 13).

It is necessary to put the finger on the asymmetrical situation which destabilizes most projects. The financial contribution comes mainly from the expatriate experts and the international agencies which naturally decide and distort the debate. For them, the reinforcement of the capacities and the participation concern first of all the recipients. This asymmetry is sometimes worrying when we evaluate the colossal sums invested in certain development projects and the negligible results. By seeking the true causes of the African failure, professor Sylvie Brunel wrote:

"In the Sahel region: the peasant farmers in the backwaters of assistance (L'Harmattan, 1998), Marie Christine Gueneau and Bernard J. Lecomte carry themselves against the agencies of assistance and NGOs, accused of imposing on the farming communities of the Sahel their own system of values and their creed as regards development, without taking account of the real priorities of the alleged "recipients" (since it is the term used) of their programs. Contrary to the hitherto discourse, they noted, that the poor are seldom reached by the aid programmes, on the one hand because they too little organised collectively, and then because their vulnerability makes reluctant to take ricks, and finally because the programmes are most often supposed a "participation" of the recipients (supposed to facilitate the famous "appropriation" of the project by the recipients), that they seldom have the means of discharging them"[87].

Nobody has the monopoly to the key of development; nobody knows all the basic needs of the populations. There is a real need of planning to work together with the concerned actors, external expertise coming from outside to resolve difficult situations like the lack of financing and technical expertise. It is necessary to avoid using a dominating language which considers local as old fashion and backward looking.

---

87. BRUNEL Sylvie, *Op. Cit.*, p. 183.

Social integrationist approach

This approach developed during 1980s, according to Olivier de Sardan (2001) supposes taking into account the heterogeneity of all the actors in the operation of development. This approach has the virtue to establish the link, or better to bring together local knowledge and the developmental discourses:

> *"Instead of focusing itself exclusively on popular knowledge, as in the populist approach, instead of denouncing the developmental configuration and its discourses, as in the deconstructionist approach, the approach centred on the analysis of the overlap of social logics takes into consideration the relationship between these two ideas, or rather between the concrete segments of one and other, and thus takes their coming together as an object of empirical investigations"[88].*

This approach, Olivier de Sardan calls it also methodological interactionism contrary to the ideological interactionism. Here all the social interactions come into play in each development project. The anthropology of development then takes varied forms: practical knowledge, practical strategies, limiting the context project and external contribution. All these understandings aim only at one thing: consensus. Each context invites a case study in a particular way. The overlap of two understandings: on the one side the developmentalist configuration and on the other local popular knowledge are really complementary; one should not exclude the other.

This approach turns towards the recognition of diversity of the actors in all the sectors where the institutions or the agents of development intervene. The scientific ideologies and the knowledge of the people once they are put together can open up the way for the development expected in the countries of the South and must help to repair the dysfunctions of the past. The social interactionist is not yet the sought solution, because development remains a complex

---

88. Jean-Pierre Olivier de Sardan, *Op. Cit.*, p. 742

field. But it opens to us new spaces of research and interpretations. Olivier de Sardan (2001)

Our analysis of the stages calls for the question of participation in the search for development. A badly prepared project is often a failure on arrival. In our countries of the South, the leaders and the local populations have only this word in their mouth. The reality is that some of them make miserable seeing and it is the case of the Democratic Republic of Congo the ex-Zaire:

> *"According to the UNDP, a child out of five dies before the age of five. That the Zaireans are among the poorest of Africa is all the more scandalous as the time of independence their country was not deprived of social infrastructures and, especially, that it is about a fabulously rich country. Managed well, Zaire could have competed with South Africa"!* [89]

And yet, despite everything the natural resources, the economic and the social reality of Congo are very negative. Instead of progressing, this country regresses. According to the Human Development Index (HDI) published by the UNDP in November 2011, Norway is on top of the countries where one lives best and the DRC comes in last position:

> *"The countries occupying the 10 last places of 2011 IDH ranking are all in sub-Saharan Africa. They are Guinea, Central African Republic, Sierra Leone, Burkina Faso, Liberia, Chad, Mozambique, Burundi, Niger and the Democratic Republic of Congo"* [90].

All the discourses on development did not yet resulted in anything on the ground. It is time not to look at only the external causes of the lagging behind (slavery, colonisation, and unfavourable trade) which the authorities always point their finger for a long time now.

---

89. BRAECKMAN Colette, *Les dinosaure. Le Zaïre de Mobutu*, Paris, Fayard, 1990, p. 215.
90. www.undp.org/2011-human-development-index-norway, November 2, 2011, Copenhagen, consulted on 16 November 2012.

On questioning the nature of the internal causes we quickly question the approaches used which appear ineffective.

We are making the plea for the social integrationist approach which aims at social interactions of the recipients and the donors: putting together the knowledge, the means, and the needs of the populations in a participative logic to fight against poverty. The question of development will take all its meaning when we examine all at the causes at the same time internal causes (corruption, cronyism, tribalism) and external causes (unequal trade, dominating discourses of the experts) of our dysfunctions. We conclude this stage on a note of hope with Sylvie Brunel that: *"Africa today is a continent waiting for development*[91].

It will take off when its dictionary of development will involve all the social interactions and not be a proper privilege of the dominators.

II.4. Promoting the equality and the empowerment of Women

This stage of our book relates to the question of gender. Article 14 of the constitution of the Democratic Republic of Congo stipulates what follows:

> *"The public authorities should take care to eliminate all forms of discrimination against woman and ensure the protection and the promotion of their rights. They should take in all the domains, particularly in the civilian, political, economic, social and cultural domains, all the appropriate measures to ensure the total fulfilment and the full participation of woman in the development of the nation. They should take measures to fight against any form of violence to the woman in the public life and the private life. Women are entitled to an equitable representation within the national, provincial and local institutions. The State guarantees the implementation of the parity man-woman in the aforementioned institutions. The law lays down the methods of application of these rights*[92].

91. BRUNEL Sylvie, *Op. Cit.*, p. 143.
92. Article 14 de la Constitution de la République Démocratique du Congo, promulguée par le Président Joseph KABILA le 18 février 2006.

It is already a good thing that the question of gender is asked and integrated into the constitution adopted by referendum in 2006. But behind all these principles of equality emphasized by this text, are hidden all the forms of precariousness and violation of the rights undergone by women. With regard to this beautiful structure and its good intentions, it is worth noting that constraints still exist in its full application. The declarations of principle and the promulgation of the laws are not enough; it is necessary that they are accompanied by the appropriate mechanisms of follow-up and implementation. In practice there is still a long way to go in the manners, in cultural practices and the weight of customs. There is lack of integration of the Constitution and measures of its enforcement by the whole of society of the Democratic Republic of Congo.

The African social universe in general and Congolese in particular, for what concerns us in this point, is crossed by power struggles which allot to the women the role of subordinates. The dowry given by the man to the family of the woman gives him more power on his wife. There is still a low social visibility of the work of women. The access to professional work still remains for them a historical conquest. Where they are able to work, except for those who have a position of command, equal qualification is not yet synonymous with equality in remuneration.

The access of women to wage-earning is a difficult course. The division of labour is very uneven and rather gives rewarding works to men as regards women. Routine and repetitive works are reserved for women so that they reproduce the same drudgeries indefinitely: cleaning, search for wood, kitchen duties, washing the dishes and cloths, pressing of cloths, sewing, keeping children etc. Colette Braeckman observes what follows:

"At the bottom of the social pyramid, there are the women. It is on them which all feudalities rest, old or modern"[93].

The entry of the women in wage-earning is not often appreciated by men who prefer to confine them to household chores. Colette says again:

"In all the country, the obligation to nourish their family and to care for the children weighs too heavy on the shoulders of women"[94].

The most ungrateful unpaid works are reserved for women. To oblige them to care for the children is the best way of reducing their chances of earning a remunerated professional career. Those who earn some money others are frighten of them. They gained their autonomy and become emancipated. At work they meet other men. This makes certain husbands jealous because they do not accept their daily exposure to the company of other men. The remunerated work of the women is a conquest in a field which society exclusively reserves for men:

"The men deal with serious things: to earn money in cash"[95].

It is thus to men that society attributes in the first place the task of earning money: women just like children are supposed to depend on the wages of the husband. We write so that the down grading and the subordination of women are not established 'ad vitam' that is for life, like immutable dogmas within our society. The reason which pushes us to invest our self in this research is to evoke the positive values which must release and protect women and to analyze at the same

---

93. BRAECKMAN Colette, *Le dinosaure. Le Zaïre de Mobutu*, Paris, Fayard, 1992, p. 260
94. *Idem.*, p. 262.
95. *Idem.*, p. 260.

time some habits which have become structural and which persist in crushing women.

The interest of this work is thus to contribute to support the effort of women to reduce the inequalities between men/women concerning their access to remunerated work and to the law. The emancipation of women in Congolese society is a cause that we support. It is a question for us to study, inter alia, a recent happening in keeping with Congolese immigration in general: the rise amongst women who decide to leave the country to settle elsewhere.

II.4.1. Sexual division of work and subordination of the women

The sexual division of work is an old fact which is true everywhere. The Democratic Republic of Congo is not an exception on the matter. According to Roland Pfefferkorn, this concept can be understood as:

"This is the established fact of the assignment to men and women different tasks and the way in which these assignments order behaviours and individual claims. It applies to both circles of paid and professional as well as to the domestic circle. This sexual division is true everywhere, as shown by the works of sociology, history or ethnology"[96].

The researches of Guy Bernard on conjugality and the role of the woman in Kinshasa confirm a clear division in the assignment of tasks between men and women:

"The roles of the men and the women, of husbands and of wives, are clearly definite and founded on a separation between the sexes. To the man falls the duty of public life, very intense, the large farming work, such as cutting down trees, to repair the furrows, works which requires only few days in the year, the construction of the house, hunting and certain forms of fishing. The woman sees herself in charge of daily work of gardening, household chores and cooking. She supplements the needs of the production on the farm by petty trading in the market more or less close to her, where she generally at the same

---

96. PFEFFERKORN Roland, *Genre et rapports sociaux de sexe*, Lausanne, Edition Page Deux, 2012, p. 95

time sells and buys. The participation of the woman in the economic life of the household is particularly important[97].

Indeed, like everywhere else, there exist in Democratic Republic of Congo the assignment tasks in a way specific to men and women. The works of the researchers Léon Matangila, Bruno Lapika and others throw light on the tribes and ethnic groups of the province of Bandundu to the south-west of the Democratic Republic of Congo. These works make it possible to understand their localization, the history, and their social organization, political, economic and cultural. The researchers show clearly that in these entities just like in the rest of the country, the work of men is distinct from that of women. There are specific tasks exclusively for women and activities exclusively masculine. They write for example that with the Boma people in the territory of Bagata,

"Women take care of the farms, the household chores and the pottery. There exist also women who are traditional medicine practitioners. The men go hunting, fishing and build the houses"[98].

With the Cokwe people who came from Angola and who were part of the Lunda empire in the last third of the 19th century,

"The men do hunting, a very important activity despite little outcome. The hunting is done either individually or in a group. The people practise hunting by net, with the hunting spear, with hunting dogs, by bush fires as well as by traps. The women do the gathering which is cantered on looking for caterpillars, vegetables and fish"[99].

97. BERNARD Guy, « Conjugalité et rôle de la femme a Kinshasa », in La *Revue des Etudes Africaines,* Vol 6., No. 2(1972), 261-274

98. MATANGILA MUSADILA Léon, Lapika Bruno et alii, *Le paradoxe politique : une réalité pour la diversité culturelle au Congo-Kinshasa. Le cas des ethnies de la province de Bandundu,* Paris, L'Harmattan, 2007, pp. 37-38.

99. *Idem.,* p. 43.

With the Lunda people, an ethnic group which is found in the provinces of Katanga, Kasaï-Occidental, Kasaï-Oriental and Bandundu,

"Hunting is done by the men in the savannah; fishing most often the work of the women"[100].

In connection with hunting with the Yansi people who are located in the territories of Bagata, Bulungu, and Masi Manimba in the district of Kwilu, the researchers write:

"Hunting is exclusively a male activity. It is done day and night, in group or individually. They practise the bush fire system as well. They set traps to catch games. Gathering is the prerogative of the women and the young girls. The gathering consists of collecting of mushrooms and caterpillars"[101].

In the division of labour as described by these Congolese researchers on the ethnic groups and the tribes of the province of Bandundu, we note that hunting is an exclusive male activity which is done individually or collectively. It is an activity practised during the day, but it is done especially at night. One needs much bravery to face the obstacles of the invisible world. Such courage makes hunting a valued activity, for this reason it is exclusively reserved for the men. To the women are reserved the household chores, gathering and work on the farm.

This division of the labour is at the same time a social hierarchical and stratification system to the detriment of women. Our observations confirm the conclusions of Mirjana Morokvasic who affirms that there exists on the international level well established

100. MATANGILA MUSADILA Léon, Lapika Bruno et alii, *Op. Cit.*, p. 72.
101. *Idem.*, p. 191-192.

traditional standards which privilege men and which reserve for women subordinate and ungrateful work:

"Sexual and ethnic division on the international level assigns women to precarious employment in socially devalued sectors of economic activity"[102].

Facing certain situations, by the weight of the customs and the culture, women are more vulnerable than men. In Congo, they endure nowadays, a form of alienated social relations characterised by exclusion, discriminations, many inequalities which are oriented to social downgrading. In some cases, women are excluded from the share of properties after the death of their husbands. The concept of sexual division of work appeared initially in France. But it is true and applies everywhere under rather elaborate principle of hierarchical and separation by through work. Helena Hirata and Danièle Kergoat saw it right by pointing out the following:

"The sexual division of labour, concept appeared in France in the Seventies, thus appears completely operational in African societies: this form of social division of labour arising from social relationship between the sexes, has as characteristics the priority assignment of men to the productive sphere and women to the reproductive sphere as well as, simultaneously, the capture by men of the functions with strong economic value (political, religious, military, etc)"[103].

The hunters who are exclusively men are part of the class of the initiated ones, with a perfect knowledge of the visible as well as the invisible universe. Hunting is traditionally a valued activity

102. MOROKVASIK Mirjana, « Le genre est au cœur des immigrations », in FALQUET Jules et Alii, *Le sexe de la mondialisation. Genre, classe, race et nouvelle division du travail*, Paris, Presses de la Fondation nationale des Sciences politiques, 2010, p. 106.

103. HIRATA Helena, KERGOAT Danièle, « Division sexuelle du travail professionnel et domestique, Brésil, France, Japon », in *Travail et genre. Regards croises France-Europe-Amérique Latine*, Paris, La Découverte, 2008, pp. 197-209, p. 199.

because the hunter nourishes his community and is part of the close collaborators of the chief. We intend to show here, without claim to exhausting the subject that through the sexual division of labour in Congo, especially in rural areas, women still undergo servitude either modern or old. In town, despite the persistence of inequalities, there are some timid improvements as regards for example the schooling of girls, a domain in which rural areas are even more underprivileged than urban environment.

Contrary to what occurs in town, many factors in rural environment (weak schooling of the girls, the weight of the traditional practices and cultural resistances, poverty, curse weighing on women without children) made Sylvie Brunel to say that:

"Women continue to live like their mothers"[104].

The weight of certain customs and traditions continue to delay the total integration of gender issues in the development agenda. The confiscation of women's rights to land and the violence by men within the family constitute a genuine barrier to social progress and to development.

In the villages, the State has not yet managed to connect households to either running water and electricity networks. Only 9% of the Congolese have access these amenities. David Van Reybrouck gives a distressing report of the state of affairs:

"The four big cities of the country are thus Kinshasa, Lubumbashi, Kisangani and recently Mbuji-Mayi. At the moment, they are connected between them neither by railroad nor by asphalt roads. The Congo can count, at the beginning of the third millennia, less than a thousand kilometre of asphalt road. Boats from Kinshasa to Kisangani spend weeks to arrive"[105].

104. BRUNEL Sylvie, *Op. Cit.*, p. 133.
105. VAN REYBROUCK David, *Congo. Une histoire*, Arles, Actes du Sud, 2012, p. 31.

This immense African territory with an exceptional natural wealth is violated by her destiny and knows only tragedy without end. At each turning point, writes Colette Braeckman,

"One thinks that the worst has passed, that the Belgian coloniser will do better than Léopold II, than independence will reduce the colonial yoke, than Kabila, the one who brought Mobutu down, will put an end to the exactions and that Kabila son will do better than his father. Alas, plundering after plundering follow one another, are superimposed, and are never ended.[106]*"*

The history of Congo is thus furnished by infinite indignations, an accumulation of the sufferings: the slave trade, colonisation (this plague which ravaged our land), dictatorship, rebellions, politician-plunderers in coat and ties, a giant without an army to defend herself. Before such a complete failure of the State where the wheel only turns too quickly and where the economic situation is saddled with corruption, cronyism, catastrophic tribalism, the population is among the most poverty-stricken in the world. The country is on her knees and cited everywhere as an example of a bankrupt country.

This country corroded by precariousness increases the painfulness of women to whom household chores are entirely given to do. It is to them and to the children that falls exclusively the most ungrateful task of searching for and fetching of water, of fire wood. In the town, despite an appearance of progress, where the women seem to be more emancipated than in the rural setting, we shall show that modern day village feudality linked to farming activities, an important sector which employs women have been transformed in tools of social discrimination against women in the house and in their professional life.

In the town inequalities still persist. Inequalities simply take other forms: it is poor women and most often young girls from the countryside who do the most socially dehumanised tasks that the

106. BRAECKMAN Colette, *Vers la deuxième indépendance du Congo*, Le Cri et Afrique Edition, 2008, p. 169

well-to-do do not want to undertake. In addition to women/man inequalities there appears in the towns as a discouraging division women/women which creates a demarcation line between richer employers who are women and poorer women at the service of the upper class, oppressed, exploited and downgraded by the richer ones. Roland Pfefferkorn has also made a similar observation in France that the opposition of the classes between women is rendered possible by the economic and financial resources difference. He noted the following that:

> *"The situation of a part of women disposing of economic, cultural and social resources is clearly opposed to the other part, increasing more and more who find life difficult and are becoming poorer"*[107].

This renders complex the understanding of the social downgrading of women when some among them take the "traditional" place of men in order to perpetuate the structures of inequality which contribute in advancing the negative message according to which women should be second class citizens.

In this part we are going to take the questions which have to do with patriarchy, the value of women's work, the work of "care" in the towns. We shall analyse also some constrains in the application of gender issues linked according to us to poverty, to the weight of some customs and some traditions, to religions, to women themselves who oftentimes have no confidence and who underestimates their own capacity and competences, to men who do not want to lose their superior class privilege and think of dominating and would want to have a blind submissive woman in front of them.

---

107. PFEFFERKORN Roland, *Inégalités et rapports sociaux. Rapports de classes, rapports de sexes*, Paris, La Dispute, 2007, p. 357.

II.4.2. Patriarchal reports

The concept of patriarchy is the product of capitalism known as a system or mode of production. According to Pfefferkorn:

"The patriarchy aims precisely at giving an account of the fact that men, as a social group, always hold the power over women in spite of the changes that have occurred during the 20th century"[108].

In this work, we will use this concept to give an account of the domination and the exploitation undergone by women from the hands of men in Africa, and particularly as in Democratic Republic of Congo. We note here that sometimes for women, emigrating from the Africa continent is a good. This escape of poverty is accompanied for them by a process of transformation of their social world. They seek to build margins of freedom and action in their new living environment. They become aware of the extent of an injustice which remains and continues to be perpetrated since time immemorial. They simply wish, as a revenge, to take over their own destiny and to recover control of the individual and collective initiative of which they have the feeling to have been dispossessed in Africa and in the Congolese speaking about the case which concerns us.

Congolese women try to denounce the hidden violence of the social relationships men/women in the light of free expression found in the West. The gender identity of Democratic Republic of Congo is produced by the social relations and the weight of the habits and manners which oblige women to be subservient. The rule of law with laws which protect and which are put in application to guarantee the status of women is almost non-existent. With regard to the institutions and customs (for traditional rights and the modern positive law), all do not prescribe in the reality of the facts than making women minors or their total dependence of men. One can read with Goli Kouassi that the 'council of elders' which is the

---

108. PFEFFERKORN Roland, *Op. Cit.*, p. 242.

traditional body the most widespread on the continent, does not concede any deliberative seat to women:

"If a customary institution is well-known in African traditional milieu, then it is well that of 'the council of elder'. Sovereign body on the level of the social group concerned, this council deliberates on all the vital questions: the source of a calamity by oracle; the designation and nomination of the village chief, tribal chief etc. A woman did not have the right to sit at this council; and if her opinions were sought, they were in a consultative and not in deliberative capacity[109]."

We continue unfortunately to live in a society completely divided in two: supreme in its masculine half and subordinate in that known as weak and feminine. One governs and controls all the power apparatus, and the other, subjected, tries to inform the whole of humanity about the persistent discriminations in spite of the existence of laws which unfortunately are late in their application.

Following cues from Amartya Sen who estimates that freedom is the ultimate end of development, Fatou Sow analyzes in a relevant way the tests which the patriarchate imposes on the participation of African women in development. Against this system, she denounces contours of the heavy traditions which leave women on the margin of freedom:

"The unequal relationships between the sexes cannot be differentiated from class inequalities, from caste and from race. The relationships between man-women are moulded in the norms emanating from the culture that religion reinforces. Whereas the society, the culture and the religion, even the law, give authority to the man, women must negotiate theirs. Today, women more openly call into question the patriarchal forms of political power and of the State which restrict their rights to citizenship, as well as the control of broad resources by men"[110].

109. KOUASSI Goli, *La prostitution en Afrique. Un cas : Abidjan*, Abidjan, Les Nouvelles Editions Africaines, 1986, p. 29.
110. SOW Fatou, « Idéologies néolibérales et droits des femmes en Afrique »

In Democratic Republic of Congo, the daily practices of gender find their roots in the customs, the traditions, the prejudices and in certain doctrines which, in the course of time, have taught men to behave as chiefs and women like subordinates and the service of men. The Congolese sociologist Albert Muluma notes that women are in the situation of permanent dependence as much in their own family as in their marriage homes. We will try to show that in several areas, the equality between man and women is not yet obtained:

> *"An unmarried woman is, in all the ways, in a situation of dependence with regard to her parents. She lives under the authority of the members of her family and the family grants her protection. At the time of her marriage, she passes under the control and the protection of her husband or that of the parents of the husband. In fact, from her dependence on her parents, she passes under that of her husband"*[111].

The patriarchate that we denounce is precisely this "putting in minority" of women. It is degrading and has become almost structural. It makes of the woman the being guided and protected by the men. This social downgrading of women is tolerated by the whole of the society.

Behind the voluntarist image not to leave woman alone without male control, is hidden on the one hand the malevolent supremacy of a chauvinist society which gives power to men, and thanks to their force, to be the only ones with the abilities required to protect women. On the other hand, it conveys the idea according to which women are unable to deal with themselves. Understood like that, the patriarchate gives to the men prerogatives: right to certain cares of the home, right over the woman. Sometimes our Congolese society

---

in FALQUET Jules et Alii, *Le sexe de la mondialisation. Genre, classe, race et nouvelle division du travail*, Paris, Presses de la Fondation Nationale des Sciences Politiques, 2010, p. 249.

111. MULUMA MUNANGA Albert, *Sociologie générale et Africaine. Les sciences sociales et les mutations des sociétés africaines*, Paris, L'Harmattan, 2008, p. 175.

in the process of development still places women under tutelage of taboos and a masculine hierarchy (patriarchate) traditionally very heavy on women. Such a system did not up till now enable them to affirm their dignity or to decide their destiny freely. There is a form of tension between the need to advance towards more autonomy and the strong place which the patriarchate still holds in mentalities. We do not want to assume the debate which divides sociologists around the patriarchate with the risk of moving away us from the framework under which we intend to use the term and to adapt it to this work. It is advisable to retain what was indicated by Roland Pfefferkorn that:

"The concept of patriarchate was criticized because of its general form, it's a-historical character, and its quasi absolute determinism which leaves few margins of manoeuvre to individual and collective subjects and consequently few possibilities for changes"[112].

The concept of patriarchate is criticisable, we no doubt about it. Other synonyms like gender, gender relationships and social relationship of sex can claim to best to explain it. What is essential to us is to start with the general proposals that Roland Pfefferkorn point out from the analyses of Christine Delphy on the patriarchate "to contextualise" them if it is the case of the oppression and the exploitation of Congolese women:

"1) The patriarchate is "the system of subordination of the women to the men in contemporary industrial societies; 2) this system has an economic base; 3) this base is the domestic mode of production"[113].

---

112. PFEFFERKORN Roland, *Genre et rapports sociaux de sexe*, Lausanne, Édition Page deux, 2012, P.26.
113. *Idem*, p.27.

If in contemporary industrial societies the mode of subordination of women passes through the economy and domestic production as Christine Delphy affirms it, in the Democratic Republic of Congo, the bases of the practices of gender emanate from traditions and customs. We can affirm with the historian Joseph KI-ZERBO that the economy of pre-colonial Africa was based on patriarchal relationships which exploited the work of the women:

"It was said that, women constituted a particularly oppressed category. Admittedly, the African woman was sometimes a working hand and a source of additional hand in the field of polygamous man. She constituted sometimes a good of exchange, being useful by her devolution in marriage, to consolidate social relations"[14].

The patriarchate as a system of subordination of women in Democratic Republic of Congo is an approach which is not the product of a biological destiny; it is a social construction which aims at putting forward male supremacy in the public sphere as well as in the private sphere. We take as an illustration this declaration of Anne-Marie Nsaka Kabunda during her intervention at the 12th General Assembly of the Council for the Development of Social Science Research in Africa (CODESRIA: Council for the Development of Social Science Research in Africa):

"The DRC is not often mentioned as a success story with regard to the question of women in political leadership. The main actors in politics and the processes of decision making are always men, in spite of the presence of women. The questions about the political programmes of women are neither exposed, nor regarded as priorities. The fact that men prevail in the public and political sphere in DRC means that its organisation and its structures are strongly influenced by the masculine values, attitudes and priorities. Very few political parties concentrated on important matters concerning women.

---

114. KI-ZERBO Joseph, *Op. Cit.*, p.176.

The fact that the DRC is a patriarchal society also reflects in the political parties and their lack of clear programme concerning the problems of women. We see a patriarchal State whose principal goal/aim is to maintain and defend such a power, an institution by the men and for the men[115].

Where Anne Marie Nsaka Kabunda accuses the patriarchal State, we appeal to return at the base, to the true source of the social inequalities i.e. to the family which, in Democratic Republic of Congo extends from the household to the family and marriage. In other words, there is in the family restricted or nuclear (the cornerstone of the social structure comprising of the father, mother and the children), but there is also the extended family (which is composed of several nuclear families fulfilling the functions of religious, economic and political community of which the village is the basic structure).

Today, even if our cities resemble people of various origins, they were built in the beginning on the ethnic basis, the first occupier of a district selling the land to those coming from his clan. The city before modifying or transforming the mentalities of the village used to be laboratory of reproduction of those from villages. It is thus within the family entity seen within the Congolese context (ethnic group, tribe, clan) which is necessary to search for the roots of the gender tree. Three points of the patriarchate seem to slow down the emancipation of the women: rights granted to the men by marriage, the rights of the parents over the children, and the cultural character of access to land by marriage.

---

115. NSAKALA KABUNDA Anne-Marie, « Espace public, espace masculin ? Politique et Genre en République Démocratique du Congo, » in *COSIDERA* 12ème Assemblée Générale tenue à Yaoundé du 7 au 11 Décembre2008, pp3-4.

II.4.3. Privileges granted to men by virtue of marriage

To begin, here is what the constitution of the Democratic Republic of Congo says on marriage:

> *"Each individual has the right to marry the person of his choice, of the opposite sex, and to found a family. The family, the basic unit of the human community, is organized so as to ensure her unity, her stability and her protection. It is placed under the protection of the public authorities. The care and the education to be given to the children constitute, for the parents, a natural right and a duty which they carry out under the monitoring and with the assistance of the public authorities. The children have the duty to assist their parents"*[116].

In the conception of marriage, the Constitution of the Democratic Republic of Congo has the merit of putting love between men and women in the centre of their union. It privileges parity and the equality. This just and beautiful notion of the monogamous marriage, of a free union without any pressure, of the space of realising unconditional love between two people of opposite sex, remains a difficult axis to follow by some polygamous men.

The polygamous aspect that the new Constitution avoids talking about, poses us a personal problem. This characteristic which threatens the dignity of the woman deserves to be examined. One cannot uphold the requirements of freedom, equality and parity, and at the same time put under the bushel important matters that this complex situation raises. Through polygamy, the condition of the woman is appreciably deteriorated, connected by the dowry, the absence of freedom and all the constraints which maintain them as subordinates. Polygamy is really unfavourable to women and children. On this subject Natacha Ordioni writes this:

---

116. Article 40 de la Constitution de la République Démocratique du Congo, promulguée par le président Joseph Kabila, Février et 2006.

"The institution of polygamy contributes to build relationships of distrust between co-spouses, relations intensified by their situation of dependence and the competition which is established between them. The status of the children of the different wives is often uneven – a survey conducted on young girls out of school in three districts in Abidjan, ("Young girls out of the school system, who are they") reveals that a good number of them were confronted with conflict family relationships registered in polygamous unions"[117].

Polygamy is a manner of downgrading wanted by the patriarchate system for the subordination of women. It grants less powers to them:

"Beyond the diversity of the particular customs of each ethnic group, there existed in Black Africa a traditional type of family which the studies of ethnologists clearly made possible to show. One can characterise the African marriage by a certain number of features. It is legitimised by the payment of services against other services at the time of ceremonies during which the two extended families reciprocally engage themselves; it is extra-clan and often intra-tribal; it has as the foundation procreation, it is potentially polygamous and dissolvable; the woman, generally very young at the time of her marriage, does not have the same rights as the man; it (marriage) prescribes sexual conducts, fixed domestic economy, the sexual practices varying considerably from one ethnic group to another"[118].

Guy Bernard touches on the complexity of marriage in Black Africa, but he faulted in trying to generalize it. Without emphasizing the specificity of each people of the continent, he informs us of assertions, of categories too vast and disparate. Which is the meaning of marriage in Congo? It is a very difficult question. To answer it, we made use of the sociological researches which agree on

117. ORDIONI Natacha, « Pauvreté et inégalités de droits en Afrique : une perspective « genrée » », in *Monde en Développement*, 1/2005 (No129) pp.93-106. URL : www.cairn.info/revue-mondes-en-developpement-2005-1-page-93htm. DOI : 10.3917/med.129.0093.
118. BERNARD Guy, *Op. Cit*, p.261.

the issue. Can we accept the simplification to the new Constitution which describes it as a free union between two people of opposite sex in order to found a family? It is not so simple like that! This homogeneity wanted by the Constitution should not make us forget the great cultural diversity of the country. The Congolese sociologist Albert Muluma could direct us well in the direction of what is the consensus:

> *"Marriage is not only the union of a man and a woman, but an alliance between two families or groups of parents. This is where the idea of counter-gift and counter-payments come from. This alliance can go until the exchange of goods received to acquire another wife. The notion of the bride price for the woman is a complex one. The concept should not be simplified, but to replace it in the whole of system of which it is an element"*[119].

The concept of marriage is really very complex in Democratic Republic of Congo. The services required in the dowry are sometimes very important. Today, we have the feeling that girls are sold by their families. Large sums are required from the husbands before the marriage. We are misusing the symbolic act which dowry is supposed to be. Traditionally, it should not be perceived as a form buying the woman. She represents a strong manner of transfer, the woman passing from the parental control and protection to the control and the protection of her husband. This transfer of control poses problem because it puts forward the inferiority of the women who are always under male supervision. Marriage grants the husband certain rights and, as we will see with Albert Muluma, it is still the man, as the only captain within the couple who receives in most cases more services of the woman of which he ensures protection on the other hand:

---

119. MULUMA MUNANGA Albert, *Op. Cit*, p.176.

"Marriage gives the husband and his family certain rights. Right to certain household care (over the person), right over the woman, right to claim any damages for injuries caused to him. It is by the dowry compensation that this transfer of right is made. Very often the husband has in fact the right to ask for divorce. The value of the woman was often the function of her fertility"[20].

In the Democratic Republic of Congo, the value of the woman remains still fundamentally related to fertility, which removes from the new Constitution the concept of a free union between the opposite sexes that it has introduced. In rural areas, the polygamous man feels strongly wealthy by the farming work of his wives and his/her many children can brings to him. And in a city like Kinshasa, to have several women is often perceived as a signs of success and of wealth.

The notion of procreation is a point which puts directly in conflict marriage called "free union" and the Congolese matrimonial customs. The confrontation is at the level of the fertility which must be ensured by the woman.

To be really effective on the notion of the marriage, the new Constitution should not be unaware of the question of polygamy. It has the duty to de-masculine mentalities and take into account the Congolese traditional reality which initially emphasises physical rejuvenation, fertility, procreation and wealth. The family is the production and consumption unit characterised by the concept of relationship which extends through the concepts of linage, clans and tribes. This does not exclude that objectively the Congolese traditional mentality is called into question and should allow itself to be informed by the vision of the new Constitution.

To have children is a pride in Congo, a continuity of the descendants/generation, a blessing. Not to have children is very badly seen: a sterile couple is marginalised and is the object of criticism and of malicious gossip. For this reason, the traditional marriage

---

120. MULUMA MUNANGA Albert, *Op. Cit.*, pp.175-176.

always presupposes procreation and fertility. But to make fertility the condition of possibilities of the union between a man and a woman is to make obstruction to the foundation of marriage which is nothing but unconditional love of man for his wife and vice versa. Marriage under the condition of procreation is a constraint which blocks the free assent of the couples.

It is not thus unreasonable to try to take hold of what constitutes the essence of the exclusion of the sterile woman: the barren womb is a curse of nature which only serves to eradicate the name of the ancestors and the continuation of the clan. The name that the Bantus (the majority of the population of the Democratic Republic of Congo) give their children is a sign of resistance against death. The sterile woman is predestined to be forgotten after her death: she is a social non-being. Mosi people (who are the Bantu people found in Tanzania and in the Democratic Republic of Congo), says Louis-Vincent Thomas, hold firmly to the continuity of their descendants:

> *"Fertility seems to constitute one of the fundamental values of the Mossi ethic for whom sterility goes "against the cosmic order". To have children and to keep them alive is an ideal to which all aspire"*[121].

Mossi like all other Bantu people, make use of procreation like means par excellence of guarding themselves against eternal death. In Bantu belief, children constitute the expression of life after death of the parents. Each birth is welcomed by big celebrations in the family. The child achieves the extension of the clan and of being. Authors like Dominique Zahan conceive the child in the Bantu thought like the repetition of the history of the species:

> *"The child is mediator on the social plan: he is the link between maternal and paternal uncles, between generations, ancestors and those alive, between his own parents and his grandparents. But he is mediator still on a much deeper basis: he indeed represents the inchoate state of humanity: he is the*

---

121. THOMAS Louis-Vincent, *La terre africaine et ses religions. Traditions et changements*, Paris, L'Harmattan, 1980, p.31.

human being considered in his origins, in his beginnings. Each child repeats the history of the species so to speak"[22].

Whereas elsewhere, in other cultures, it is understood that couples can make a choice not to have children, with the Bantu people, marriage is recognized by the two families only with the birth of children. It is still the case nowadays. Sexuality is not an individual act. It is above all a social act which concerns all the clan. A customary marriage with the Bantu people does not rest primarily on love but on the foundation of a family. A marriage without children is inconceivable in the Bantu tradition. The union between the man and the woman presupposes and aims at ensuring fertility. And if this requirement is not met, the union has either to be dissolved, or a remedy to be found. The lack of children in a couple opens up the way for polygamy. The man cornered by his own people will seek a second wife to ensure an offspring. A sterile marriage is a disaster which ends unfortunately either in a divorce or by a second marriage which creates a polygamous home.

In this matter, still today with the Bantu people, it is the man who decides. Concerning the descendant, the opinion of the woman does not count. Polygamy lived as a search for offspring does not shock anyone. It gives to the man the right to take a second, then a third wife if possible so as to leave a descendant. Those who have many children appear in the Bantu mentality like parents truly accomplished. In rural areas, children constitute a free labour for the parents. They ensure the future on the economic level and confer prestige and especially social consideration to their father.

Polygamy thus ignored by the Constitution of the Democratic Republic of Congo proves strongly how much our society remains marked by the patriarchal system, and how the political community itself is embarrassed by this question. The equality between men and

---

122. ZAHAN Dominique, *Le feu en Afrique, culture et cosmologie*, Paris, L'Harmattan, 1995, p. 31.

women will not be translated in the facts, except that day when the men who hold the keys of power will agree to question the rights they have granted themselves by the tradition and the custom.

The right of the parents over the child

It is not a matter here of the alternating custody of the child by divorced parents. We want to briefly approach a fact which is nothing else apart from the construction of our society largely based on the patriarchate which deprives women and children of their rights. Whereas women devote all their existence to raise children with affection and devotion, they actually have no or very little rights with respect to their children. The dowry is paid to the father of the girl or to the maternal uncle of the girl according to the patrilineal or matrilineal system of membership of the child.

The truth is this: in the two systems, the men are the only ones to control the rights of the children to the detriment of the women:

The rights of the father over the child differ from one society to another. In the matrilineal system, the rights of the mother, or more precisely of the brother of the mother, are of everyday usage[123].

The rights of the parents over the children come in fact to the father in a patrilineal society. On the other hand, in the matrilineal society, it is not the mother, but her brother who holds the power. The maternal uncle is the chief, it is him who determines and directs the activities of the clan and he takes care on all the members of his group. It is him who marries off his nephews and nieces. Towards his maternal uncle, the child has the same respect as towards his own mother. Everything is done so that the woman is dependent on the man and feels the incapacity to take any initiative without the help of the man. Behind what can appear like a complementary help of

---

123. MULUMA MUNANGA Albert, *Op. Cit.* , p.176.

man/woman, of brother/sister, of husband/wife is hidden a societal process of downgrading of the woman:

"It is in the relationships of brother-sister and man-woman that the society locates the necessary complementary help of the man and the woman. The division of labour between the two sexes makes in such a way that the woman without the man, whether her husband or her brother, she is a helpless person"[24].

There are no complementary helps between man/woman, brother/sister, there is an unjustified fear to promote the empowerment of woman because the dowry has already paid for the rights of the woman. There is a major injustice with regard to the women. They give life, they protect the children and at the end of the day they do not have the same rights as their husbands on the children. In mentalities of the Congolese, the common law (customary law) is stronger than the Constitution.

According to Natacha Ordioni, an investigation conducted by the Congolese ministry of Social Affairs and the UNICEF (1999) reveals that:

"62% of the Congolese are married under the customary law. The wife then does not have any right or recourse in the event of repudiation, of divorce or death of the husband, and her children are generally entrusted to the guardianship of the paternal family, in accordance with the process of segmentation of linage. The investigation still reveals concerning the DRC that the ignorance of written laws and the negative representation which surrounds it push women to resort to the (customary law) common law in a proportion of 70% to solve conflicts"[25].

---

124. VERBEEK Léon, *Contes de l'inceste, de la parenté et de l'alliance chez les Bemba (RDC)*, Paris, Éditions Karthala, 2006, p.28.
125. ORDIONI Natacha, *Op. Cit.*, pp 93-106.

The common law (customary law) has a great influence on the daily life of the Congolese and because our traditions utilise the visible as well as the invisible world in the application of sanctions, when the rules of life are transgressed. It is an inclusive vision of the world which includes the ancestors, the living and the children to be born. At the foundation of the patriarchate, the men succeeded in making the women admit, by the means of the customs and of our traditions that the almost exclusive rights that they granted over the children come from the ancestors. The ancestors are not dead; they take care on the harmony of the living. There is the life after death. It is necessary to be a good person so as to enter into the hereafter, if not to be condemned to wander on earth.

The women, in towns just like in the countryside, give excuses to advance their rights which are violated or confiscated by the men, except for some here and there which take individual initiatives or in women associations who make significant moves.

In addition, there is weakness in the application of the sanctions envisaged by the new Constitution against the attacks on gender against women. Any law is ineffective when it does not envisage exemplary sanctions against any person who ignores it. The texts are there and, as long as the lack of parity and equality will not be condemned, women will always be underestimated by men. Moreover, in a Congolese society still dominated by orality, the Constitution (written positive law) suffers a lack of popularisation and appropriation, whereas common law (customary law) is known by those in charge of each clan, tribe and ethnic group who make sure they are respected. The coexistence of these two legal systems is not favourable to women. Here we would like to make the following point: between orality and written form of expression we do not see complete boundary. Between the two, there is mutual and permanent encounter that serves as a data base to history as a science.

Cultural character of the access to the ground by the marriage

It is a question of denouncing the disadvantages which arise from the exclusion of Congolese women of the possibilities which men enjoy concerning their access to land and landed property. It is advisable to update the discriminations which reduce the access of the women to land and to show how marriage is still used for their subordination. The weak representation of women in politics makes very complex the resolution of the problem. Meanwhile, the inequalities resulting from the patriarchate and the common law (customary law) continue to make difficult the free access to land title for women. Natacha Ordioni informs us of these inequalities:

"The subordination of women is also in direct relationship with their material dependence. In sub-Saharan Africa, the common law (customary law) does not acknowledge the same rights of access to land to the two sexes (Goody, 1976; Boserup, 1983). When the transmission of land is patrilineal, the women are excluded from land heritage and even their right of usage is conditioned by their marital status. The women generally do not benefit from the right of usufruct on land of their husband.

A second provision contributes to exclude women from the access to land: in DRC or Namibia, the woman has an official status of a minor and must obtain the prior approval of her spouse before concluding a contract. Legal norms being still dominated by the principles concerned with the common law (customary law), they contribute by the very fact of things (de facto) to exclude women from owning land. Also women farmers produce 80% of the food in sub-Saharan Africa but own only 1% of the land"[126].

Access to land by Congolese women is still linked to marriage. It is not uncommon to find in DRC that this right is taken away by widowhood. After the death of a husband, the children and the wife are often stripped of goods and the house and even the right of usufruct enjoyed by women stops from the moment death takes

---

126. ORDIONI Natacha, *Op. Cit.*, pp. 93-106.

away the husband or at the moment the couple separates in the case of a divorce.

II.5. The Value of Women's work in the Democratic Republic of Congo

In the Democratic Republic of Congo just as elsewhere in the world, women have always worked. It does not matter whether it is in town or in the village. They contribute seriously to the welfare of the family as well as to the development of the economy of the country. Work is good for health as well as social status. Here, we shall try to show the cultural parameters which lead to discriminate against women in relation to work and which make visible the social inequalities in the society. In the Republic of Congo, there is on the one hand those who underestimate women's work, hence refuse to acknowledge women's work, and on the other hand those who do not allow women to access remunerated professional jobs just because the society wants to confine women to work at home as housewives.

This can be observed from our interview with Jerome (61 years) and his wife Marie (58 years) by Florent Alain BIKINI, the author.

Question to Jerome – if you were younger, would you have allowed your wife to access a professional job with salary?

Answer of Jerome: My wife has passed the age of getting a job; she is just at home selling little charcoal. Yet even if we should have been younger now I will not allow accessing a professional job; many office women are prostitutes or are unfaithful to their husbands. They often sleep with their bosses.

Answer of Marie: It is not good for a married woman to work with another man, the temptation is very high. It is very common with our young girls[127]."

---

127. Extrait de l'entretien entre Florent-Alain BIKINI (l'auteur) et le couple Jérôme et Marie le 08/08/2013 dans la commune de Mont-Ngafula à Kinshasa, RDC.

So it is still very common, those who are hostile to women's access to offices. For most of the women, professional work with salary remains an historical conquest. Let us show how the instrumentalising of gender issues does not favour women's access to office work. In the rural areas, agriculture, intimately related to domestic activities remain the major activity of women. Hence, before we touch on what concerns the work of women in urban areas, let us clarify two points: women in agriculture and women in domestic activities.

II.5.1 Women with Agriculture: the case of the North-Kivu and South-Kivu Provinces.

We choose to talk about the North-Kivu and South-Kivu Provinces and the one of Maniema situated in east of the country because they are essentially agricultural provinces and are also densely populated. These regions situated on high altitudes are on the one hand safe from many diseases, and on the other hand very good for cattle raring. Its soils and climate favour the production of valuable cash crops such as tea, coffee, and quinine. Unfortunately, women of those regions are not only weakened by hard farming but mostly by the war which expose them to the phenomenon of rape at all the time. According to Collette Braeckman, for long time ago, things are not changing in Congo namely: women remain true pillars of the family. More and more with no help from anybody they ought to work hard and take care of their children's, health, education, food in the house, all on their own effort. They work all the time in order to satisfy all these needs.

Congo has been very instable and this has lasted for many years. All started from the failure of industry and the suspension of international aid to the DRC with the dramatic consequence of looting everywhere in the country, destroying here and there small and medium businesses. Such situations led to the breaking down of the whole economy of the country during the reign of Mobutu around 1990, later followed by the war of 1997. These crises were made worse by the instauration of multi-party system by Mobutu. His promise of economic revival turned into a catastrophic situation. According to David Van Reybrouck:

"At the end of 1974 Mobutu passed into "radicalisation". Suffering enterprises were all nationalised. They could continue to work to generate enough income that he could use to satisfy and retain his friends. The social consequences were sad. Mobutu was a good communicator but a bad economist. The fiasco of Zairianisation increased unemployment in the country"[128].

The Zairianization was a bad system of governance, a dishonest system according to which enterprises and industries were taken away from expatriated people and handed over to those near to the centre of power. With bad management, the situation became unacceptable. Economy instability was very spectacular. The process of 'zairianisation' contributed to a high inflation and many industries were close up. From the middle of 1980, the IMF, and the World Bank, desirous of reducing public expenditure and the cancellation of imposed some financial discipline through the policy of the Structured Adjustment Programme (SAP). According to Collette Braeckman, the Zaire of Mobutu;

Zaire was the first country in Africa to put into practice the policies of structural adjustment[129].

This was a real fiasco. The social consequences resulting from the austerity measures were deplorable: patients and parents were obliged to pay for their health care and even for the education of their children. As for the socio-political situation, it can brief be stated as follows: five years of instability from independence until Mobutu took over the reins of power by a military coup d'état (1960-1965). His term will be marked by thirty two years of bad management (1965-1997). Then the term of Kabila, father and son,

---

128. VAN REYBROUCK David, *Op. Cit.*, p. 384.
129. BRAECKMAN Colette, *Op. Cit.*, p. 23.

will be marked by nineteen years of civil war from 1997 up till today. This long time of instability was caused by an abusive exploitation of mines of the country(with the biggest part of the cake given to China without any parliamentary control) and especially the fact of using women on the battle field.

Woman who became prisoners of different rebel groups were the first victims of various kidnappings and rape. Colette Breackman gave us a sense of the difficulties women suffered:

"Their stories are hallucinating: not only were they victims of several rapes, but they also suffered extreme cruel treatment. Sticks, bottles and knives have been force into their vagina. Sometimes after the rape, shots were fired; they were burnt by the explosions. Many were seriously mutilated; all of them suffered from fistula where the genital organs were destroyed and the stool is mixed with the urine. In addition to such physical suffering, they receive all kinds of humiliation: most of them were sent away by their husbands. Discouraged and tired of life they are rejected by the community. It is on them, the victims that fall the burden of the fault and all the grudges of their social group"[130].

The joblessness of the men, who were breadwinners of their families and their forced enrolment in the various armed groups, rather increased the difficult in many households and made the cost of life higher and by consequence increased the amount of work of women who made the necessary efforts to help their husbands and their children and family. In her recent book on Congo, Colette Braeckman reported what she recorded from a farmer prosaically:

"'Our wives are our ploughs'. It has been like that yesterday and even today, our wives, short and slim, climb the hills carrying twice their weight. Their eyes are drawn by a strap that supports a hood resting between their shoul-

130. BRAECKMAN Colette, *Vers la deuxième indépendance du Congo*, Bruxelles, Le Cri, 2009, pp. 189-190.

ders. When they start on climbing a slop, the women walk bent and their bodies make an acute angle with the pathway"[131].

Women work hard, to the point of being compared with tractors and ploughs. The situation of war which lasts puts into perspective, the weak income levels in families and leaves women to get the supplement. In another book, Colette Braeckman, gives us an idea of the weight that women carry each day:

The burdens weigh up to 50kg, more than the weight of this frail women always accompanied by the little children on their back[132].

They work hard on the land to cultivate maize, cassava, potatoes, banana, and groundnut... They come back from the forest or the savannah carrying fire wood on the heard, mushrooms, gallons of drinking waters or green vegetable for the family. These kilograms to carry coming back from the farm are decidedly reserved for women.

"Unchangeable on the contrary was the weight of the burden that already at the age of eight years old, little girls were supposed to learn how to carry"[133].

A young girl, sometimes to the disadvantage of her education is compelled to learn how to carry heavy loads in order to be able to serve the men. More a work is hard, humiliating and repetitive, better it is for women. The question we asked ourselves in relation to women's status in rural areas is the following: is the agriculture that women practise work to be taken into consideration? Can we really talk about work? Will it not be better to talk about it as the prolongation of domestic work exclusively reserved to women?

---

131. BRAECKMAN Colette, *L'homme qui répare les femmes. Violences Sexuelles au Congo le combat du docteur Mukwenge*, Bruxelles, Le GRIP, 2012, p. 13.

132. BRAECKMAN Colette, *Le Dinosaure. Le Zaïre de Mobutu*, Paris, Fayard, 1992, p. 260

133. BRAECKMAN Colette, *L'homme qui répare les femmes. Violences Sexuelles au Congo le combat du docteur Mukwenge*, Bruxelles, Le GRIP, 2012, p. 14.

We shall answer our question in two ways. First by choosing to support women and all the sacrifices they make, we shall say that agricultural work they do is a real work, hard but not recognised and acknowledged and appreciation by men and it's just economic value obscured.

Even if farming generates some financial resources, it is meant first and foremost for subsistence of the members of the family. The women gain nothing for themselves apart from caring for their husbands and children. This laborious activity none gratifying is for men a means of exploitation and subordination of women. Sylvie Brunel is right when she wrote:

"Farming has been devalued in the mind of people with regard to civil service work. The direct consequence of the neglect of farming is the ever increasing vulnerability of women in rural areas[134]."

Through the downgrading or the low appreciation of farming activities, there is also the downgrading of women because the large part of food needs of the family come from farming. In fact, it is a social process of domination through work. It consists in placing less value on the work of women and placing more value on the work of men and thereby overshadowing the profitability of the productive agricultural sector in the families:

"At Kivu, which is one example among the many regions in Zaire, traditional powers remain very strong. When it comes to farming for the Mwami, who is the traditional chief, it is women who are sent. Men take care of serious things: earn money in cash. But most often than not, it is wasted. Therefore the real daily subsistence remains the duty of women. It would have been more urgent to make the men, who pass their evenings, if not all their days in long palavers. But the men are interested in remunerable work only: the work of daily sustenance of the family is the work of women[135].

134. BRUNEL Sylvie, *Op. Cit.*, p. 72.
135. BRAECKMAN Colette, *Le Dinosaure. Le Zaïre de Mobutu*, Paris, Fayard, 1992, p. 260-262.

This is a discriminating mind-set through the activity of farming. The men leave for the women to do the non-remunerative part of the work which is painful and demeaning. All that does not bring financial remuneration is left to women. To them is not only imposed free service, but most of all, men do not want to accord any form of self-reliance so as to control them. Generally, men are the exclusive breadwinners of families. However, economic independence of women is not seen well by men.

II.5.2 The work of women in the domestic setting in rural areas

It is difficult to understand that the family which is the place par excellence of the expression of conjugal love, should itself be attacked by the conditioning of women from their very young age and confine them only to domestic activities as if it was exclusively reserved for them. We can find the basis of our affirmations in the writing of Roland Pfefferkorn on inequalities and social relationships. This makes us conclude right from the outset even before speaking about the Congolese countryside where the situation is deplorable, that, to different levels, according as one lives in the countryside or in the cities there exist, even now, forms of inequalities regarding the participation of men and women in domestic work.

Ultimately we can say that the most ungrateful tasks continue to fall to women even if some of them are emerging undertaking inspirational professional careers:

"More fundamentally still, in maintaining unequal relationships in the family cycle in which is shaped very early sexual identity of individuals, this division reinforces the construction of masculine and feminine models unequally valued and rewarding leading not only the majority of young girls to integrate the idea that despite everything, most of the domestic tasks – especially the less prestigious ones – will be theirs in spousal duties, but mostly to adapt in consequence their school and professional ambitions. It is ultimately also the case within conjugal and family relationships, under the cover of love, that

continues to be reproduced until now, inequalities between men and women and between classes"[136].

Congolese men actively hands over all domestic activities to women who also accept it in the name of the conjugal love. In the rural areas, parent finds it normal that it is the duty of the young girl to execute all the domestic activities while cooking at the same time, yet here and there are young boys playing all the day long. But at the end men are the one to be serve first. It is the duty of the mother to initiates her daughter in such activities in order to make of her a good housewife. For a woman who did not know how to accomplish all the domestic activities is a shame and an insult for her mother. Under such customary belief, women work all the day long without any appreciation from men.

So to speak, women especially in the rural areas are always busy. They work more and more though they gain nothing as such. And just as it is being affirmed by Colette Breackman,

> *"The best intention of the world about rural areas is that women are never free, they always have something extra to do. The day starts at dawn and end at midnight.*[137]*"*

Our analysis about women's work in the rural place comes to put emphases on two points: on one hand, the gratuity of services and on the other hand the refusal to acknowledge and appreciate how much women struggle for the welfare of the family. The power of men over women is not only from the public opinion but from the nuclear family. Just for the love of the husbands and children, women in rural areas are subjected to the strict observation of customary beliefs and practices.

---

136. PFEFFERKORN Roland, *Inégalités et Rapport sociaux. Rapport de Classes, Rapport de Sexes*, Paris, La Dispute, 2007, p. 344.
137. BRAECKMAN Colette, *Op. Cit.*, p.262.

In towns, where Congolese women are relatively free from traditional and customary belief struggle as much as they can to gain their autonomy. But it is always on them more than men the repose the duty of educating the children and to feed all the family. The economic statistics are practically non-existent. A research study done by the National Institute of Statistics, gives a detailed picture of the principal characteristics of economic activity and of unemployment in the country. They (the principal characteristics) allow us to identify in which sector of activities Congolese women are more engaged in urban areas:

> *"The national coverage of the whole research allows distinguishing the informal agricultural activities from non agricultural activities, the later, more concentrated in urban areas. They come from more than 90% production units of less than six persons, of which about 69% are self employed. Those earning salaries are very week with less than 15%. More than half of the non-agricultural informal jobs are in petty businesses and about one quarter in the service sector. The workforce in the informal sector is more of young people: more than 20% of those active in the informal sector are less than 25years old. With the level of study averaging 8years, it is also the most feminised sector, since more than one out of two in the informal sector in Kinshasa is a woman[138]".*

As the research has shown, in the Democratic Republic of Congo, *"the unemployed are about 72% of the active population"[139]*. Congolese woman work more in small businesses and services also known as the work of 'care', two sectors that we are going to analyse briefly.

---

138. MAKABU MA NKENDA Timothée, MBA Martin, TORELLI Constance, « L'emploi, le chômage et les conditions d'activité en République Démocratique du Congo : Principaux résultats de l'enquête 1-2-3, 2004-2005 », Document de travail DIAL, DT, 2007-14, p. 8.
139. MAKABU MA NKENDA Timothée, MBA Martin, TORELLI Constance, *Op. Cit.*, p.8.

II.5.3 Informal work of women in Kinshasa

"Unemployment is an urban phenomenon. Thus, one third of the unemployed Congolese are in Kinshasa (are Kinois).[140]"

The unemployed Kinois as well as those from other cities (big towns) live on the mobilised family solidarity, base mainly on money transferred by those abroad. *"Thus in almost 95% of the cases, the unemployed are taken care of by their families[141]."*

Other unemployed survive out of informal sector, an area which creates self-employed jobs and which absorbs the unemployed. By the fact of the insignificant salary of those who have the responsibility of finding a salaried job, by the fact of the destruction of the mineral sector, but above all faced with the suspension of international aid, an informal economy is the only way out. The way of functioning of this sector permit Professor Malikwisha Meni to affirm that the whole of Congolese society functions informally:

"Far from being able to satisfy the need of the less fortunate in the society, the Congolese informal economy permits to cover almost the totality of the society even those who are politically, economically and socially in better positions. It can be affirmed that the whole of the Congolese society functions more of less informally than formally.[142]"

It is a vital and unstoppable activity (of course neither taken seriously into account in the statistics nor in the calculation of Gross National Product GNP). With unimaginably small salaries, this informal sector drives the economy of the capital. Each one buys something and resells to others goods and services. The informal sector starts from selling foodstuff s to construction materials passing

---

140. MAKABU MA NKENDA Timothée, MBA Martin, TORELLI Constance, *Op. Cit..*, p. 7.

141. *Idem.*, P.19.

142. MENI Malikwisha, « L'importance du Secteur Informel en RDC », in *Bulletin de L'ANSD* (Académie Nationale des Sciences du Développement), Volume I, Kinshasa, Décembre-janvier 2000-2001, pp. 21-40.

through shoemaking, the hiring of chairs for festivals and burials, the services of Quado, the name given to those repairing tires, pans and pots, umbrellas…). Colette Braeckman describes the ingeniousness of the Kinshasa population in facing difficult situations:

"In the city Kinshasa, at Kitambo, Kimbaseke, Ngaba, have appeared small vegetable farmers and people keeping small animals. Jewellers work on gold and copper, sculptors carve ivory, artists survive by making rubber stamps, signposts for shops, true and fake portraits. In Kinshasa and also in Kisangani and Lubumbashi, in these big cities where about 40% of the population live, reigns a continuous activity.[143]"

The Congolese society is organising herself as much as she can in facing poverty. Even though there are men, the informal sector is the most feminised in the capital. The informal economy is even called *"that of women and poor of the city.[144]"*

Just as in rural areas, subsistent activities weight upon women. In Kinshasa the capital, they are the ones supporting the needs of their families. They practice informal businesses that allow them to be economically independent. In Kinshasa informal business is spreading everywhere in such a way that one has the impression of being in a market in everywhere in the street. In the poorest areas of the capital, everybody sells something to somebody.

The survival of families depends seriously on such elementary exchange of simple goods and services offered by women each day. The search for autonomy pass through mastering the financial resources, an area for a long time reserved only for men. *"They have*

---

143. BRAECKMAN Colette, *Le Dinosaure. Le Zaïre de Mobutu*, Paris, Fayard, 1992,p.266-267.
144. *Ibidem*

their small businesses, work on their ngandas (stalls), small cafeterias of the street.[145] ”

Inside one street, one will find a family selling sugar and bread, another family sells salt and soap, a third family sells cassava flour and vegetables, a fourth family sells beer and cigarettes, another family will be selling medicines without prescription another family offering communication and telephone services paid for by the minute to those who cannot subscribe to the telephone system or buy a personal telephone. The women of Kinshasa who are less submissive (than other women in the rural areas) to the traditional constrains and relatively relieved from the customary system, try their best to gain their autonomy. Conscious of their helpless situation of having nobody to help in looking after their children, they try their best in organising themselves so as to raise their heads high:

"The women and it is always they, who try their best getting something in the villages and to sell to and get small benefit from the markets in the town. The enterprising ones do the crossing over the river to Brazzaville, on the other side of the river, where they can get a better exchange in the CFA currency.[146] ”

For us, far from being the strategy to follow, the informal sector is first and foremost a way of civil disobedience. The crisis pushes everybody to look for and to get some income from somewhere. Men disobey the state which is incapable of creating jobs in order to give employment to the jobless. Those who are employed in offices also work the informal sector, without saying that it is impossible to survive with the low wages. Women are in the informal sector so as to overcome the patriarchal system which for long time has given men monopoly to control financial resources. For us, education is a social good, and not for making business, or a domain reserve for men. For women, working in the informal sector, covers their lack of

145. BRAECKMAN Colette, *Le Dinosaure. Le Zaïre de Mobutu*, Paris, Fayard, 1992., p. 262.
146. *Idem*, p. 268.

educational qualification. The maintaining of the majority of women in the informal economy is because of their lack or low standard of education. Congo is facing *"a very high proportion of women with low level of education."*[147]

Thus, it is the consequence of the inequalities of chances in the school between girls and boys, which pushes the women of Kinshasa to enter the informal small businesses in order to get their daily bread and financial autonomy. Also, because of fees going higher, there is a social discrimination which is disfavour to the formation of girls. As for the family when, because of various reasons must sacrifice the education of a child, the girls are the first victims. Congolese women are continually suffering from discrimination and marginalisation in the matter of education. It is true that women are different and do not form a homogeneous group. Yet we would like to denounce a certain form of exclusive which is called in Congo, the sexually transmissible result. This is a shameful practice which discredits some professor in colleges and universities.

This constitutes a serious hell for young ladies who are victims. From high school (secondary school) to the university some teachers ask for sexual favour as an easy way to let girls pass to a higher class. One way of humiliating these girls, has been statement such as: your head is safe only after, you are destined to be an object of sexual pleasure for men. To pass one's exam after offering a sexual favour meant admitting that one is intellectually inferior and thus replacing such weakness by valuing of feminine charm. So to reduce oneself in order to achieve the same thing as men, that is to have degrees, finishes by creating frustration on the job market.

Such sexual perversion which is creeping slowly in the educational system in Congo confirms the inequalities between men and women. There is on the one hand those who succeed by hard work and on the other hand the successes obtained by the exchange of sexual

---

147. MAKABU MA NKENDA Timothée, et alii, *Op. Cit.*, p. 39

favour which diminish the value of the feminine certificates on the job market. Sexually transmissible grades are a constraint the young ladies endure from the hands of some lecturers in colleges and universities. Such situation is not only an obstacle to the efficiency in the educational system but also gender discrimination and sadly contributes to the downgrading of women. The man/woman inequalities are structural. It is unfortunate that even the scientific world in Congo does not escape such situations. The worse is that very few voices are raised to denounce the total impunity:

"An illustration: Kinshasa, the most urbanised city of the DRC is also the city where are located the biggest universities of the country. Yet, it is in this city that the system of sexually transmissible grade (STG) was developed. Some of those who are not urban dwellers but coming from the village in order to study in the university were "forced" to accept this practice. According to Bongo-Pasi Moke Sangol and Tsakala Munikengi (2004, p.106) were clear on this situation: "... Sex is sometimes exchanged for mark. Such a deviance phenomenon, which is not only a Congolese problem, is practised excessively in Kinshasa. (...) What student themselves say about their personal success testifies to that the opportunism which underlies this poisonous attitude is spreading." This practice is becoming trivial, with an almost zero cost without any restrictive measure to counteract it.[148]"

Exchange of sex with mark is not just a deviance. It is, in our opinion, another form of perpetuating the domestic subordination of women and transplanted into the educational and academic sphere by the men. In such situation those women trying to pursue the same university education degrees like their colleagues, see themselves sadly discriminated against by men and thereby invalidating the merit of their intellectual competencies. The practice of STG corrupts many African countries. The News site (Paper) *Afrik.com*, denounces the same situation and phenomenon in the Gabonese educational

148. KODILA TEDIKA Oasis, « Anatomie de la corruption en République Démocratique du Congo », in MPERA Paper, No. 43463, Janvier 2013, pp. 1-20.

system. It is one of the reasons which reduce the education level of girls and make it a shame to be a teacher.

To solve the problem, the news site proposes that the Gabonese population should come out from their silence and do something. Thus the government of Gabon State doing something:

> *"The administration agents and those in charge of schools must listen to young girls and engage in their protection against sexual harassments. Many girls suffer in silence insides class rooms and do not dare speak out for, by the often time solidarity of the body of teachers, the students have never had a reason and to have refused a rendezvous with a teacher, the girls risk to be tagged to the extent of temporary suspension or even definitive exclusion from classes. Afrik.com wish that the Gabonese state should get involve herself in the protection of young girl in schools by the creation of an office for listening in all schools and universities of Gabon where girls in a difficult situation could go without any fear.[149]"*

It is important that African states take this issue seriously. They ought to fight fervently against this identification of women with the least social classes without any intellectual requirements.

II.5.4 Services rendered to Families/ Work of Care/Work of Domestic Helps

We are in a very complex domain. In the Democratic Republic of Congo, the work of 'care' is essentially part of services offered to individual persons or families in town and it is often the case that both the care givers and their bosses are from the same village or area. It is a system that is based on the interdependent relationship between the individuals. The contribution of these young girls employed as care-givers, (commonly known as 'bonnes' or 'house-helps') is not subject to any regulation. Their identification, simply as

---

149. MBOG BATASSI Pierre-Eric, « Les moyennes sexuellement transmissibles frappent le Gabon », in *Afrik.com* of 5 January 2008, consulted on 15 June 2013.

'house-helps', reveals the exploitation of these young girls (since girls are majority in this domain).

Bonnes (house-helps) could be identified with machines, doing everything and working all the day long without rest. There in no time set for work and resting. There is no limit of work or time for work during the day. All domestic activities fall on their shoulders; washing, cleaning, ironing, cooking, and shopping. All this is with very little salary which sometime is not handed over to the girl, the reason being that she is offered free accommodation and food. They endure the services and worse of it include sexual violence by the male employers. We noted also some prejudices against their human dignity: torture, intimidations and privation of freedom are current.

According to Margerite Rollinde, the family serves as the pretext to exploiting and helping to worsen the situation of young girls who are already in a precarious situation:

"In Africa where the work of the Bonnes (house-helps) is not subject to any regulation and or where it is heard oftentimes from women, even among intellectuals and militants, explaining that these children (it is the case of young girls of 13 and 14 years, or even younger), are part of the family. Families welcome them with good heart with their open intention to help them, but in reality they end up being over-exploited with unlimited time of work and never think about sending them to school with the children of the family"[150].

There are very few elderly homes and centres where elderly people could be welcomed in the Democratic Republic of Congo. The state has totally resigned itself from this domain. The only institutions which are in charge of caring for children and vulnerable adults are those put up for a long time by European missionaries. In most part of the country, these elderly persons are left in their families where most often young girls from villages are taken as Bonnes (house

150. ROLLINDE Marguerite, « Espace domestique, espace politique, espace économique : genre franchit les frontières », in *Genre et changement social en Afrique*, Paris, Editions des archives contemporaine, p. 5.

helps) to help them. Since these arrangements are done between the wealthy of the cities and the poor of the countryside, under the label of 'good heart', it is difficult for these young girls to denounce all the mistreatment. Silence is the master and everyone is quiet. We can notice same similarities between 'the Bonnes' (house helps) from the villages coming to work for women with a considerable economic resources in the cities and African women from the cities who travel to European countries to work for the bourgeois in the adopted countries.

There is a new realism that imposes itself on African countries: more they would like to modernised, more they are oblige to cease behaving like in the past and to search for human values (African human values) which is eluding them more and more. Our countries have to build medical units or medically quipped institutions for elderly people and those who are isolated. Values like family mutual help in caring for the elderly at home, even though a noble idea seems to us less adapted to the current evolution of society. If not we in Africa will ceaselessly continue to sacrifice the education of young girls from the village for the care and welfare of children and the elderly of those from wealthy families.

The highest numbers of illiterate women are found in Africa. Two third of women in villages can neither read nor write. In many rural areas, women continue to live like their mothers of old: low level of education of girls and mostly with the high and historic birth rates of 6 to 8 children per woman. Poverty of women and their refuge seeking in the work of 'care' speaks thousand words. As long as governments will not privilege the education of women in the rural areas, their poverty seen in trying to look for low paid jobs in the cities will only but get worse. The low level of girls going to school is symptomatic of the feminisation of poverty. The work of 'care' as it is practiced by arrangement between families will not eradicate misery but will rather aggravate the precariousness of girls. It is not a question of education between families. Here we are, in our opinion in a certain form of modern exploitation of vulnerable people by those who have the means.

"The weight of traditional practices and cultural resistances, still very heavy in the rural areas: they (traditional practices and cultural resistances) make of women 'baby producing machines' once they are married (oftentimes with men much older than them, those who can pay the dowry) and limit the practices of contraception"[151].

As long as sub-Saharan African countries do not engage in a developmental programme that takes into account women in rural areas, these women will see their lives stopped by bad treatment that the world pretends to ignore. A society which wants to be modern and marked by such changes and uncertainty, one cannot continue to forget the marginalisation of rural girls as against their access to education and not giving them any chance as becoming only Bonnes (house helps). In other words, it should be proper to fight against illiteracy. Education of girls is the best way of emancipation of men and women from the practices which do not conform to human dignity. Every bird flies with two wings, Africa will reach real development, when she gets to understand that it is both men and women who contribute to change the world.

II.5.5 School and Education

The situation of Bonnes (house helps) calls for a serious questioning on the access to school and to education. The school is a serious weapon which allows us to fight against superstitions. According to Jean-Marc Ela, education is the best way of awaking human consciousness, to fight against arbitraries, to organise otherwise and to educate:

"To equip the communities with instruments of self-defence, the practice of literacy becomes a moment of reflection on the problems of health, of food,

---

151. BRUNEL Sylvie, *Op. Cit.*, p. 134.

of farming and of the rights of the people. At the same time, the school transformed into centres of total animation for the parents who discover, as a peasant farmer once said that 'a village without a school is a village of slaves' (not being educated, is like being in slavery). Everything aims at "removing" misfortune and to render to man the ability to speak[152].

As much as the school is an instrument coming from outside, imposed by the colonial masters, many are Africans who agree in saying that education is the only efficacious way for true freedom from certain bad inclination and servitude of old and of the tradition. With education, people who are for a long time destined to ignorance opens to knowledge and reason. Education is one of the good things left for us by the colonial master.

Parent capable of paying for the education of their children are investing, putting in the means, believe in the future success of their children. Education frees.

Even though illiteracy and the lack of education are not exclusive to the people of Africa, the increasing number of people who cannot read and those who have no access to any form of education, make of the continent almost marginalised and excluded from the modern world.

Which type of illiteracy are we talking about and what proportion does it occupy in the life of Africans? It is one of the challenges little spoken about but in our opinion, it is the greatest challenge to face, a problem which casts shadow and degrade life in rural and certain urban areas of Africa. We firmly agree with Ela and Santedi that lack of education is a serious handicap for economic development of black African.

"One of the factors that increase the socio-economic crises in Africa is without doubt ignorance. About 162 millions of Africans, making more than one third of the population of the continent are totally illiterate. Such a situation pollutes other sectors of life and brings about much negative consequences

152. ELA Jean-Marc, *Ma foi d'Africain*, Paris, Karthala, 2009, p. 31

... Ignorance plays a role in the underdevelopment mentality and recourse to witchcraft as the only way of explain the causes of failure, the morbid fear of bad spirits, fetish mentality ... all these factors are found in uneducated illiterate places"[153].

In some African countries, like the DRC, this situation is growing worse. The salary of teachers in both the public and private sectors is paid by parents themselves either jobless or not paid for several months. With such a situation where more and more of our co-citizens can neither read not write because they come from modest families, we must know that millions of people especially women, are not only deprived of the basic minimum of life but worse still, deprived of speaking in a world at an era of writing.

For us, as well as for Jean-Marc Ela, the sign of millions of Africans in search for freedom and justice are so much as not to draw the attention of our leaders.

"How many illiterate people are paralyzed by ancestral and modern fears in our societies where the accumulation of new knowledge is the order of the day according to the elitist model? Let us observe that ignorance is not limited here only to reading and writing: it extends to the functioning of political institutions, to the economic mechanism, and to the laws in the society. Before such multiple harassments and blind bullying of which they are victims, the illiterate masses of the African countryside go as far as to ignore the laws that protect their rights"[154].

The political leaders today can no more close their eyes from the ignorance of the people they are leading. We cannot totally come back to oral tradition since the will to develop Africa is been seen everywhere. Education of the people becomes a priority, a real need that DRC should face. While we wait for better days to come, millions

153. SANTEDI Leonard, *Les défis de l'évangélisation dans l'Afrique contemporaine*, Paris, Karthala, 2005, pp. 45-46.
154. ELA Jean-Marc, *Le cri de l'homme africain. Questions aux églises d'Afrique*, Paris, L'Harmattan, p. 48.

of women are deprived of their elementary right to education. Charlemagne, the king of France did not totally invent the school, but he remains in the collective memory as such, as some historians think, as the one who made education available for all. In Africa, that such a dream will become a reality one day! That is our greatest wish. In the present situation, it seems to us unjust to deprive from the access of education and the right to equality those who do not have the chance to go to school. A new and an adequate policy must be invented to take really such marginalised people into consideration. The equality that we are asking for is not the biological differentiation between the sexes, men is always different from woman biologically. We are militants for the deconstruction of the structural and cultural inequalities which come about as a result of the patriarchal system in the DRC.

II.6 Future Perspective

Thinking development with Women

To rethink the development of the country (DRC), women ought to be at the centre of poverty reduction programmes. The role and the status of women are better indicators for potential of growth and development of any nation. According to two great York Times reporters, Nicolors Kristof and Sheryl Wudunn, we think that discriminations wherever be their origins, do not have to be accepted as fixed elements determining a particular society:

> "If we believe firmly in some values, such as equality of all human beings, it does not matter the colour of their skins, or their gender, we should not be afraid to defend them. It will be irresponsibility to accept slavery, human torture, the tying of the legs, the crimes of honour or excision for the simple respect of the faith and the culture of the other"[155].

---

155. KRISTOF Nicholas et WUDUNN Sheryl, *La moitie du ciel. Les femmes vont changer le monde*, New York, 2009, Poséidon Press, Paris, Editions de Arènes, (Traduction française), 2010, p. 334.

To bring about an effective empowerment and emancipation of women is very difficult in the Democratic Republic of Congo. The issues touch patriarchal practices themselves. They chock the culture and the well established family structures, they disturb the laid down customs. Will it not be better to imitate the neighbouring Rwanda which originally characterised by the very patriarchal society and poverty, but which with the implication of women in political decisions and economic life on the national level, now shows an unbelievable growth rates?

"From such a poor and infertile land came out a nation in which women play henceforth an important economic, political and social role from which all Rwanda draw some profit. Rwanda favours empowerment and the promotion of women: probably that is what explains the fact that Rwanda is one of the nations which shows rapid economic rates in Africa. In many things – except her smallness –, Rwanda has become the new China of Africa... The constitution states that women ought to take up to 30% of seats in the parliament"[156].

Strengthened by the example of Rwanda that is near to us, we all know with many more examples that no culture is immutable and that transforming it for the betterment of all people is never a disfunction but rather transformation and improvement. It is undeniable that the transformations which has started in the Congolese couples in and around Strasbourg are motivated by what Albert Muluma calls a new social psychology:

"The social psychology wants to establish the conditions and the ways of life of people as a psychological reality that is growing from individuals who gather together. Interaction and communication become the essential elements.[157]"

In addition to the fight against poverty, openness to new ideas is something that pushes Congolese in Strasbourg to desire success. We

---

156. KRISTOF Nicholas et Wudunn Sheryl, *Op. Cit.*, p. 340-341.
157. MULUMA MUNANGA Albert, *Op. Cit.*, p. 126.

cannot deny them the fact that they are capable of the strength to work for profound changes of the practices and behaviours within the couple, it is true. We cannot underestimate the fact that the determining factor of the transformation at work in them is their interaction with the society in which they find themselves is at the origin of the dynamic of change.

Our development ought to pass through a kind of deliverance from our own blockage, by destroying our masculine domineering opinion and rethinking and by giving more value to the place of women in our society. Our culture must reorganise itself in view of the future in term of total interdependence. What social actions should we adopt today in order to assure every Congolese his/her part of initiative and creativity? The Congolese philosopher KÄ Mana envisages human existence as the power of innovation and principle of transcendent creativity.

"A new beginning is always possible, that a new-born is always to wait for, for humanity itself is power for new beginning.[158]*"*

The new things capable of transforming the social relationships between men and women in the Democratic Republic of Congo in particular and in Africa in general are not destructive of our social fabric. They are rather signs of human capacities of initiating and creating and enhancing the freedom of invention in Congo of tomorrow.

We shall insist with Nicholas Kristof and Sheryl Wundunn on the power of transformation of education:

"An uncountable number of studies show that education of girls is one of the most effective means of fighting poverty. Oftentimes, it is also indispensable to allow women to stand against injustices and to be integrated into the economy. As long as they cannot read and write, it will be difficult for them to

---

158. KÄ MANA, *L'Afrique va-t-elle mourir ?*, Paris, Les Editions Cerf, 1991, p. 21.

create viable enterprises or to contribute significantly to the economy of their countries"[159].

The task of the political leaders of the present Congo is to make sure that education becomes effectively a right of each child neither discriminating between the sexes nor social classes. Even of the impact of education is difficult to estimate in statistical terms in a country as huge as the DRC which can count only 20% to 25% of usable roads; we however, still hold dear the good value that, the education of girls will bring prosperity to our country. This idea rekindled the hope of Kristof and Wudunn that:

"The arguments in favour of the education of women are still convincing. We know many women because of schooling have gotten good work or were able to create businesses, and transform their lives and those of their neighbours. More generally, it is admissible that the prosperity of eastern Asia since some decades no is due notably to the education of girls and their integration into the workforce – a phenomenon without equal in India and Africa"[160].

To educate many girls in Congo should make them more profitable in the long run thanks to economic impact that this human capital, mostly left on the sideline, will contribute to generate. In the situation of injustice concerning the accessibility of girls to education we have to bring our social conscience back as a nation because the imbalance will set back more our development.

II.6.1. *Professional activities of Women*

We have seen in the first part, how sexual division of labour reserved for women le roles least satisfying and mostly repetitive and without much remuneration. Work is the area in which men and women confront themselves on the one hand to claim domination and on the hand to look for autonomy and emancipation. It is truly the tool that men have used for a long time to enslave women. In

---

159. KRISTOF Nicholas et Wudunn Sheryl, *Op. Cit.*, p. 281.
160. *Idem.*, p. 282.

many family situations nothing is given in advance for the women. The simple decision to leave one's husband and to go and work, even if no longer a taboo, is a way of going against the husband.

Two structures, capitalism and patriarchy[161] , according to Pfefferkorn Roland have used work as the lever of domination. Still today, women use this tool as a medium to reclaim what has been taken away from them:

> *"Work is an essential lever of domination. But if the emancipation of women has known some successes, since more than a century and most of all from the 1960s, it is necessary to insist that it is also because of work. It is mostly about the sexual division of labour or of the recognition of the competencies considered as natural "qualities" (that it is not necessary as a result to pay according to their just value) that women have arrived at fighting, to stage strikes actions, from the 19th century"[162].*

Congolese women, by mostly informal business, have taken the same lever by which men have downgraded them, to come out of the domestic space to enter into the public, so as to mobilise themselves and to take their emancipation into their own hands. Today in the world, the social recognition passes through work. A demarcation line has henceforth been drawn between those who work and those who do not and those who are looking for work.

There are on the one hand those who make the economic machine of the country to work and those who depend on the sweat of the others. It is really difficult to be a jobless person these days. As a

---

161. For Pfefferkorn, the concept of capitalism as a system of production is at the origin of the elaboration of the concept to patriarchy which aims to give account of the fact that men, as a social group, hold always power over women despite the changes which about in the 20th century. Pfefferkorn Roland, Inégalités et rapports sociaux. Rapports de classes, rapports de sexes, Paris, La Dispute, 2007, p. 242.

162. PFEFFERKORN Roland, *Genre et rapports sociaux de sexe*, Lausanne, Editions Pages Deux, 2012, pp. 117-118

result, according to Pfefferkorn, work participates in France in the construction of the feminine identity:

"The work of women has become a massive social fact. It is henceforth written in the social reality and all indication is that, it has become an irreversible phenomenon"[163].

The work of women, an irreversible phenomenon in France, is still a domain to conquer in Congo. Surely work is an important tool of emancipation which frees, which empowers, which is good for the health. But should one accept any type of work so as to gain her autonomy? The floating salary status simply means that there is no regulation which can open the doors to abuses of all kinds: salary domination, exploitation of the various vulnerabilities, silence imposed by subordination and the status of an employee (in need) and employer (the one who gives work) which finishes in the overlooking of the work done.

These women found themselves again in the same form of allegiance which was necessary in their proper domestic sphere. This is what makes us to question the extent and the importance of the changes taking place. At this point we doubt that the immigration of Congolese women is not oriented to the desired results: that of the integration in the welcoming countries and empowerment and equality in couples. The quality of their employment indicate a tendency to polarisation between, on the one hand, the superior professions reserved for men and the women of the welcoming countries and on the other hand, the low salary employments which have become henceforth the area for the women of immigration. There is certainly transformation of social relationships but there is also no eradication but rather the displacement of inequalities.

In the Congo, the informal economy of women among the poorest of the city has no statistical references. In the Western countries,

---

163. PFEFFERKORN Roland, *Inégalités et rapports sociaux. Rapports de classes, rapports de sexes*, Paris, La Dispute, 2007, p. 323.

their mode of economic insertion (clandestine work and in areas less paid) render their role invisible.

II.6.2. *Sharing of domestic work*

In the DRC, it is not so much the concern of society of the fact that it is still the duty of women who take care of the kitchen, wash the dishes, wash the cloths, and do the ironing and the sewing. It is even normal, as it can be noticed in the interviews (between Florent-Alain 'F.-A.', Sidonie 'S.' And Henri 'H.') conducted recently in Kinshasa, that these tasks are the domain of women:

> F.-A. – *Good morning Sidonie. Which of you take care of the household chores?*
>
> S. – *Good morning. I am the one to do everything*
>
> H. – *We are in Congo, it is the woman who does the household chores.*
>
> F.-A. – *Sidonie, if you have the possibility to make Henri work, what will be the reaction of your neighbours?*
>
> S. – *I will be criticised.*
>
> H. – *It is true that it's the woman who accomplishes these tasks. Personally, I am disposed to doing it. Once I even tried to do my own washing. The angry reactions of the neighbours ask that I stop doing what is for women[164].*

Marie (Mary) is 51 years old and Jerome is 68 years old are more categorical that the man cannot undertake domestic chores:

> F.-A. – *Congolese women in Europe are asking for more equality in families and in public. They want to be treated as men. For example, to let the men also undertake some domestic chores: bath the children, do the cooking, washing the dishes... Have you thought about it?*

---

164. Extract of the interview between Florent-Alain Bikini Musini and the couple Henri and Sidonie at Kinshasa on 2 August, 2013.

Jerome – No, these women are exaggerating. We have to respect our customs and the Holy Bible itself said that woman came out of man. They are not even equal. We have to stop that thinking. Man cannot wash dishes, that no and big never! I have paid the dowry, I earn money to look after the family, and do you want me to prepare my own food?

Marie – These women are exaggerating. It is the men who must lead us, we the women and not the opposite. I cannot make my husband a laughingstock to that extent.

F.-A. – For you then it is not possible and you do not have this idea in your head. However, if other women incite you to do it, would you do it once you arrive in Europe?

Jerome – In no case at all! Never, that would not happen.

Marie – Impossible! Besides with our age nobody can force us to change our habits. A man cannot undertake duties reserved for women.

F.-A. – Without hiding anything, how old are you?

Jerome – 61 years.

Marie – 58 years[165].

This inequality in the domestic roles within couples seemed not to have worried the men we have interviewed. The entire domestic does inevitably come to women. In Strasbourg and her surroundings, Congolese women fight on many fronts for the transformation of social relationships with their husbands. By work, education of their girls and informal businesses, they are giving birth to a new culture. Things are more complicated in the domestic sphere where, like their counterparts in France, Congolese men participate very little in making the domestic tasks reserved for women a bit easy. They

---

165. Extract of the interview between Florent-Alain Bikini Musini and the couple Jerome and Marie at Kinshasa on 08 August, 2013.

do it not because of the need of equity but simply like an occasional assistance to their wives. Just to mention that despite the resistance of men, women are beginning to raise their voices to fight for their rights.

We see it in the kitchen, in washing the dishes... these little progresses will pave the way for better days which were culturally unthinkable. The welcoming country herself has a long way towards an equitable sharing of domestic chores:

> *"Visibly for women, coming together as a couple increases the amount of domestic chores. The presence of children, especially little children, implies an inevitable increase in household chores. But these chores fall notably to women. In other words, the presence of children increases considerably inequality in sharing domestic chores"*[166].

Even if raising little children can appear as a natural disposition predestined for women by breastfeeding among others things, we can also see in the lack of or little implication of men in changing diapers for example as a wished manipulation to keep certain privileges of the dominant sex. For us, men and women should apply themselves with more ardour in reducing inequalities in social relationships.

The domestic sphere is the incontestable place for the balancing to be done. It is in the family that the breaking away from stereotypes that we know can be done: cooking and the household chores of girls, studying and do-it-yourself jobs for boys. We have to put the family at the centre of the fight against inequalities in the sexual division of labour so that as early as possible the boys and the girls appear without complex in accomplishing the same or similar tasks.

---

166. PFEFFERKORN Roland, *Inégalités et rapports sociaux. Rapports de classes, rapports de sexes*, Paris, La Dispute, 2007, p.330.

II.6.3. Eradicate the practice (tradition) of dowry

With the weight of the dowry, women find themselves in situations of permanent dependence. There is dependence in relation to their own parents in their families of origin, and dependence in respect of their husband and the parents of their husband once they form couples. What appears as protection of women is nothing rather than confiding them to the house and not allowing them to grow humanly speaking. This is a way of saying that they are incapable of taking charge without the control of men.

This downgrading of women is structural and is tolerated and accepted by the whole society. How can we then make changes and also expect improvement? How can we question the social relationships based since time immemorial on gender differences? This the big question which has guided our reflection in this book, that which has allowed us to understand that Congolese women suffer in silence, accept without challenge the established order and capitulate.

By this book, we became conscious that we are contributors to a society dominated by patriarchal relationships which give more prerogatives to men and which by that very fact is less favourable to women. Giving equal chances to men and women of our countries is an effective way to stimulate our economic development.

Marginalisation of women sacks our desire to succeed away. And so, the country find herself deprived of workforce and of talents of the majority of the population. There surely a link between the suppressing of women and the progressing underdevelopment in our country. In all the countries, the role and the status of women are considered better indications of the growth potential and of development. The DRC would gain much and would not loose anything if her leaders would come out with a political will to put women at the centre of the development preoccupations. Apart from the polygamy, it is true to say that the act of marriage itself is in the very beginning unequal with on the one side the man who disburses today huge sums of money to buy the services of the woman and on the other side that of the woman who must render in the name of love and gratitude what was paid for her. The dowry is what makes equality unthinkable. We can say many times that it is only a symbolic compensation given to the family of the woman, however, the abuses show clearly that for the families it is oriented to a very lucrative business. The very high cost dowry bills for some men, like Formant, whom we have interviewed, justify the use strong reifying language towards women:

F.-A. – what do you have to say on the subject of dowry?

Formant – As regards a dowry, I would say that it is the price that men pay for women to belong to him[167].

When the free consent and the exchange of man/woman romantic sentiments of love are conditioned by the fore payment of gifts and money, we do have the formation of equal couples enjoying the sae rights and duties towards each other, but we come necessarily to a subordination of the one from whom the love is bought. Dowry renders impossible all idea of equality man/woman in the head of a large number of Congolese men. Pierre (Peter) whom we met at Kinshasa speaks his mind openly:

"It is not possible. The woman remains a woman and the man is the head of the household whatever means the woman might have and her professional situation. I cannot tolerate that the woman considers herself equal or above the man"[168].

We support the abolition of the dowry to allow men and women to enter into marriage as equal partners free from all forms of external

---

167. Extract of the interview between Florent-Alain Bikini Musini and the couple Formant and Gracia at Kinshasa on 25 July, 2013.
168. Extract of the interview between Florent-Alain Bikini Musini and the couple Pierre and Ida at Kinshasa on 10 August, 2013.

coercion. The access to land and to some resources through marriage is a source of much suffering for women in the DRC. There is no worse subjugation of a woman than the duty to wait for the survival from the good will of the husband. If the husband dies, which often is the case because the life expectancy of women is more than that of men, knowing that the women are married much younger than the men, they find themselves totally abandoned as sad and single widows in the street without resources and with children to feed.

II.7. The dream of the future: Partnership

For a long-time African have remained prisoners of a sad history that, unconsciously however, maintained them under her tutelage. The salvation of the Black man is not in international aid and help, domination and subordination. It is in the freeing process from this mentality which makes to believe that we do not have anything to offer and have to receive everything. It is the time, more than ever to make peace with ourselves and with our past.

It is time that the door of no return becomes that by which African Americans and all blacks in the diaspora will come back to invest on their ancestral home. Bravo to Ghana, to Cameroon and to Senegal who have made the administrative procedures simpler to facilitate the coming back of those who would wish to. It is time that Africa and the West learn to become true partners.

The only remedy against the fragile insecurity is the valuing of work and the mobilisation of the people for a better and equitable distribution of resources. The equitable distribution of resources should denounce the inequality between the citizens and update the bitter reality that we all make a widespread sentiment, that there is a justice for the poor and another justice for the rich. We have to expose the seriousness of the issue of corruption which touches and shakes all the sectors of life and above all to fight the trivialisation and impunity of perpetrators.

Conclusion

Our vision for future generations ought to take root in our successes and also taking account our failures. What Africa need today is to free itself and make itself available for any transformation that is being proposes by her children. On such a way to freedom and a new type of world to invent, Leonard Santedi thinks that *"of neither desperation nor pessimism can be justified in relation to the future of Africa and other poor regions the world"[169]*.

We ought to try with all we have at our disposition, to invent and to create the future for a rebirth of our continent since this is the way forward:

"Since the 15th century, Africa has experience together with the Western world a violent and tragic encounter which went up to nineteen century. If such an experience has a certain attenuation consequence of the physical violence, the symbolic violence on its part has remained untouched it is because of the pains attributed to it for such a long time. And even today, Africans continue to experience such a violence which we could notice through their language even if the principal actors are not conscious of it (...)

Nevertheless, above all pains of especially Africans, there seem to remain something common to both the slave trade and the colonisation: Something common that may not be perceive directly or even sometime rejected by some Africans as well as some Europeans. Such commonness starts by history, no matter how tragic it was. Whether it started on the beaches of Elmina in Ghana or that of Ouida in Benin, the presence of old canons as well as old castles – French, Dutch and Portuguese – witness not only the rivalries between Europeans powers of the time of the slave trade but also commonness of history How can one refuse such a common history"[170]?

169. SANTEDI KINKUPU Léonard, *Les défis de l'Evangélisation dans l'Afrique traditionnelle*, Paris Karthala, 2005, p. 120.
170. SOME Roger, Préface to *Hermitage Silencieux*, Catalogue of the exposition organised by the Masters degree Students of the University of Strasbourg, Metz, Editions des Paraiges, 2014, p. 5.

How to make such a common history with the Western countries a haven of peace? This work is an invitation to Africans to stop searching for the escape goat elsewhere. It is a prompting to work and to scientific production. And to arrive at it, the school is the best tool not to be neglected if we want to get out of the isolation and to bring the African touch to the community of nations. We are equal because we are different; it is equality in difference. The affirmation of our cultural heritage and our creative liberty, this is what Africa wants to share with the rest of the world. We have to remain ourselves and acknowledging the other and his/her need to be different. It is the time for Africa to create and to refuse to copy blindly a lifestyle which is foreign her own.

This work is an attempt which does not pretend to be exhaustive. The sentiment within us is the one of discussion started which needs to be followed and re-actualised in Africa. Our wish or dream is to see in a near future in Africa especially in Lagos, in Dakar, in Bamako, in Yaoundé, in Kinshasa, in Abidjan, just to mention most of our countries from which the greater number of the young 'exiles' come from, a general state on the youth sacrificed by clandestine immigration. May the voice of Africa be heard at last, in a way that something else may be proposed to the youth rather than the clandestine immigration towards Europe.

Such a cry ought to reach the ears of all in the situation of dependency and to shout it louder to them that it is the time to stand up and raise up the head. The youth are questioning us and we have to heed to their pain. The West was not built in a day and that its wealth is a result of a hard work. We have to stop leaving under tutelage. Our determination to come out of poverty and underdevelopment is the only hope for better future among other nations.

Credible institutions, rigorous universities, specialised school; these are for us indispensable tools that Africa needs not to neglect on the way. Resource persons must be appointed in the education sector and they have to teach the students and researchers to embrace a continental value. To fight against illiteracy in a world that is becoming more and more civilized, each one of us ought to make sure he or she watches over the education of children and also ask various governments to take education as part of their national priorities.

The identity of African does not play in her isolation but rather in intercultural exchanges. African ought not to evolve in self-centred communities like the cast system which does not integrate with others.

This work of analysing the past of Africa must not take the form of judgment against the West which is largely white whom, for some, the heroism the generosity towards Africa is not to prove. As an example, here is a testimony of a missionary who came back from Africa.

> "I experience something from that transforming power, within me when I arrived as a young missionary in Cote d'Ivoire. I was preaching the gospel and celebrating mass as if I was before Europeans.
>
> I was proud to transmit all the knowledge I have learnt. For this cause I was staying four or five days in the villages. I was gathering sympathisers who come to listen to the Good News and also for prayers. For the first time a big crowd gathered around me. But after some time I realised that the number of listeners and faithful was reducing considerably and I realised that I was having only the same faces in front of me. They explain to me that they hardly get right what I was preaching despite the fact that I was wasting their precious time for farming. But since they did not want to frustrate me, they always delegate some people to be there for me and listen to me.
>
> Then I questioned myself: Will you still stiffen on your practices, your knowledge, and your imported habits from outsides? Will you require them to become a photocopy of your culture and of your church, by asking them to leave their being, their sensitivity, their culture? The consequences of such a

situation will be a great obstacle to their effective human and religious development and will surely lead to a one sided integration, to a kind of another tower of Babel. I therefore decided just like Jesus of Nazareth, to incarnate myself as much as I can despite my limitation, inside the culture of the people. I started learning everything, how to sleep on a mat, how to eat their food, how to bath with a bucket of water behind a tree, how to speak their language, to adapt myself to their way of working and relaxing.

In fact, I experienced a real death-rebirth. And I was rewarded because one day the traditional leaders came to me and said: "you, you will never go back to your home, you will remain with us. Here are parcels of land for you to farm, there is a new house built for you, and here is a wife for you. Make your abode with us". I explain to them that I was well pleased with their propositions but that all I did among them was to remain with them even if it is not material or charnel, it is still human and religious. As such I continued my mission among this people for twenty five years, participating in their fight for justice, freedom, development, dignity, for good health, against illiteracy and against all kinds of discrimination and dehumanization, of division, hatred and death.

The victory of Jesus will be manifested especially through the transformation of our interpersonal relationships. I cease to be the superior, the servant, or the Christian in front of pagans. I became rather a human brother, who in the name of his faith in Jesus Christ refused to simply live among them, but who was living with them. Since they were well invested in a kind of the language of imagery, they also show to me that they appreciated such a change. One evening, while playing with children, an old man who was looking at me said to his neighbour "I would have never dreamt that one day a panther will play with my children!" My friend Simon explained to me later that, the panther is the only wild animal which can kills for pleasure, without eating the victims.

That is the image of the way in which the colonial master was imposing himself on this people in order to dominate the country for decades, no respect for laws and the right reason. But villagers have now come to realise that even the white panther could, leaving himself to be transformed by the victory of Christ. Do you not think that such an experience, though singular, can help us to reflect and if a white man can change, an African can also change.[171]"

The challenges facing African (under development, sicknesses, ignorance, lack of means to satisfy basic needs, wars, brain drain) give the impression as if the continent is a marginal one. Should we give the impression of a bad conscience, losing hope and discouraged about the future of our continent? No. For us, our continent is simply one with varied realities that we need to clarify her problems in order to understand its differences and its particularities. Her history, her conception of the human being, of life and death, her ancestral practices need to be comprehended.

It is necessary to try to understand the mentality, the culture and the philosophy of African, for we can only develop people if only we are capable of understanding them. It is important to know that Africa has her own dynamism which is proper to her especially when it comes to her relationship with the world.

The importance of respect of cultures finds its real meaning here. Each culture is a coherent whole which are different from other cultures and which we ought to protect. It is true that there is always in human being such a tendency to be attached to one's roots, the need to find a matrix of one's humanity, a need to find security only in one's environment because the only values, the only messages having a true impact on the people are those which bring human beings together to feel at home. We have to discover the human values that permit to reduce tensions and conflicts, and which safeguards human dignity and respect of others.

The history of humanity is all about the need to love and to be loved. The most wonderful foundation of hope is to know that

171. This is a testimony of Fr Jean-Paul Eschlimann of the SMA on his return to Alsace after 25 years of his life in Cote d'Ivoire.

others need me and that I cannot do without the help of others and their need.

Before planning a new beginning for our continent and to lay the foundations, it will not be appropriate to attribute the mistake or the causes of our problem to others, that is to say to the West, but to acknowledge on all levels our responsibility in order to promote new reforms for a better future.

Will we ever be totally freed from all implication in the corruption and impoverishment of our own people? Should we always point out only to the Europeans? According to Léonard Santedi, it is worth to acknowledge our own mistakes.

> *"It is the obligation of the truth towards ourselves, in as much as, "the failure of Africa", is less economic than human. We must be very sensitive to that side of our responsibility as Africans in our own history. A critical reflection will lead us not to spare a word, not to use any euphemism so as to criticise this childish attitude which consists in endless claims of our integration into an international network, while revealing our incapacities of managing what we have or the little we receive.[172]"*

As Africans, we are the first to complain, because we have betrayed the trust that has been put in us. It is now time to raise our heads and to stop wasting our time in obsession of the past not very glorious. Facing the static situation in which African finds herself trapped in, it is worth affirming with Achille Mbembe that even the decolonization of Africa simply seemed as a noisy accident, a dry surface noise or again the sign of a misled future. The past is no more; let us think of the future so as to resurface on the good side.

> *"What then holds this delirium, and what are the more elementary behaviours which reveal them? First of all that the Black Man, is this person (or again that person) that we see when we see nothing, when we understand nothing and, above all, when we want do not want to understand anything.*

172. SANTEDI KINKUPU Léonard, *Op. Cit.*, p. 64.

Everywhere that he goes, the Black Man liberates passionate dynamisms and provokes irrational exuberance which always puts to the text the system of reason. Thereafter, the fact that nobody – not even those who invented him, not even those who decked him with this name – want to be a Black Man or in practice to be treated as one. Of the others, according to Grilles Deleuze, "there is always a Black Man, a Jews, a Chinese, a Big Mongolian, an Aryan in the delirium" since what brews delirium, among others things, is the race.

In reducing the body and the human being to something of belongingness, to a kind of skin and colour, attributing to the skin and to the colour a fictitious biological status, the Euro-American world in particular made of the Black Man and of race two sides of the same coin, that of codified foolishness. Operating simultaneously as an original category, material and fantasy, race was, in the course of previous centuries at the origin of many catastrophes, the cause of untold psychic devastations and numerous crimes and massacres[173].

Achille Mbembe is inviting Africans to come out of the models which the western conquest has enclosed them in. The destiny of the continent and her history remain without expression in the imagination of western society in a present with failure. We ought to free ourselves from the imageries that are retarding us. It is thus within human consciousness that we ought to look for the need of our raison d'être of today. The present time or moment disappears very progressively. Yet is a disappearance which gives birth to other moments which are also destined to disappear. To exhume a sense which wonders in the past, that is to say, a sense devoid of the present in itself, is difficult. There is in time a sort of permanent absence. It is a futile exercise to exhume the past in order to understand it. The

173. MBEMBE Achille, *Critique de la raison Nègre*, Paris, La Découverte, 2003. pp.10-11.

present, even if unstable, is always there as an image of eternity in time.

To advance, the human will goes through a time of crisis. There is in every human person an interior struggle between two different wills. In this struggle comes time as a possibility of understanding the interior distortion. Time represents a painful experience of rapture/separation between intended destination and our wondering in time. Time make sense only at the moment of human decision for or against goodness. Africa, it is time for you to make a choice for goodness.

BIBLIOGRAPHY

Abbé PIERRE, *Testament...*, Paris, Bayard, 1995.

ACHEBE Chinua, *Le monde s'effondre, présence africaine*, Paris, Dakar, 1972.

ADOUKONOU Barthélemy, *Jalons pour une théologie africaine. Essai d'une herméneutique chrétienne du Vodun dahoméen*, Tome II : étude ethnologique, Paris Éditions Lethielleux, Namur culture et vérité, 1980.

BACHELARD Gaston, *L'intuition de l'instant*, 1932.

BEECHER STOWE Harriet, *La clef de la case de l'oncle Tom*, Adamant Media corporation.

BERNARD Guy, « conjugalité et rôle de la femme à Kinshasa », in *La revue des études Africaines* », Vol 6.N° 2 (1972).

BRAECKMAN Colette, *Le dinosaure. Le Zaïre de Mobutu*, Paris, Fayard, 1990.

BRAECKMAN Colette, *Vers la deuxième indépendance du Congo*, Le cri et Afrique édition, 2008.

BRAECKMAN Colette, *L'homme qui répare les femmes. Violences sexuelles au Congo le combat du docteur Mukwenge*, Bruxelles, Le GRIP, 2012.

BOVE Laurent, « Lumières « radicales » ou « modérées » : une lecture à partir de Spinoza », *ESPRIT* n°357, Août-Septembre 2009.

BRAHAMI Frédéric, « L'empire divin des préjugés. Joseph de Maistre contre l'esprit éclairé », *ESPRIT* n°357, Août-Septembre 2009.

BRUNEL Sylvie, *L'Afrique*, Rosny-sous-Bois Bois, Éditions Bréal, 2004.

CÉSAIRE Aimé, *Cahier d'un retour au pays natal*, Paris, Présence africaine, 1983.

COQUERY-VIDROVITCH et alii, *Être esclaves. Afrique-Amériques, XVe-XIXe Siècle*, Paris, la Découverte, 2013.

DAMBISA Moyo, *Dead Aid. Why aid is not working and how there is a better way for Africa*, New York, Farrar, Straus and Giroux, 2010.

DANIEL Serge, *Les routes clandestines. L'Afrique des immigrés et des passeurs*, Paris, Hachette, 2008.

DOUMA Jean-Baptiste, *L'immigration congolaise en France. Entre crises et recherche d'identité*, Paris, l'Harmattan, 2003.

ELA Jean-Marc, *Ma foi d'Africain*, Paris, Karthala, 2009.

ELA Jean-Marc, *Le cri de l'homme africain. Questions aux églises d'Afrique*, Paris, l'Harmattan, 1993.

ESCHLIMANN Jean-Paul, *Les Agni devant la mort*, Préface de Louis-Vincent Thomas, Paris, éditions Karthala, 1985.

FERRY Jean-Marc, « Les Lumières : un projet contemporain ? », *ESPRIT* n°357, Août-Septembre 2009.

FOESSEL Michaël, « Refaire les Lumières ? », *ESPRIT* n°357, Août-Septembre 2009.

FOTTORINO Éric et alii, *Besoin d'Afrique*, Paris, Fayard, 1992.

GUITTON Jean, *Le temps et l'éternité chez Plotin et chez Saint Augustin*, Paris, Vrin, 2004.

HOCHSHILD Adam, *Les fantômes du roi Léopold. La terreur coloniale dans l'État du Congo 1884-1908*, Paris, Éditions Tallandier, 2007.

HIRATA Hélène, KERGOAT Danièle, « Division sexuelle du travail professionnel et domestique. Brésil, France, Japon, in *Travail et Genre. Regards croisés France-Europe-Amérique latine*, Paris, La découverte, 2008.

Jean-Pierre Olivier de Sardan, « Les trois approches en anthropologie du développement. » In: *Tiers-Monde*. 2001.

KÄ MANA, *L'Afrique va-t-elle mourir ?*, Paris, les éditions du Cerf, 1991.

KANT Emmanuel, *Réponse à la question : Qu'est ce que les lumières ?*, traduit de l'allemand par Jean Mondot, Presses universitaires de Bordeaux, 2007.

KELMAN Gaston, *Je suis noir et je n'aime pas le manioc*, Paris, Max Milo, 2004.

KI-ZERBO Joseph, *A quand l'Afrique ?* , Paris, éditions de l'aube, 2003.

KODILA TEDIKA Oasis, « Anatomie de la corruption en République démocratique du Congo » in MPERA Paper N° 43463, Janvier 2013.

KOUASSI Goli, *La prostitution en Afrique. Un cas : Abidjan*, Abidjan, les nouvelles éditions africaines, 1986.

KRISTOF Nicholas et WUDUNN Sheryl, *La moitié du ciel. Les femmes vont changer le monde*, New York, 2009, Poséidon Press, Paris, Éditions des Arènes, (Traduction française), 2010.

LATERGUY Jean, *Les guérilleros, Jean Lartéguy sur les traces de Che Guevara*, Paris, Presses Pocket, 1967.

MAKABU MA NKENDA Timothée, MBA Martin, TORELLI Constance, « L'emploi, le chômage et les conditions d'activité en République Démocratique du Congo : principaux résultats de l'enquête 1-2-3, 2004-2005, Document de travail DIAL, DT, 2007.

MATANGILA MUSADILA Léon, LAPIKA Bruno et alii, *Le paradoxe politique : une réalité pour la diversité culturelle au Congo-Kinshasa. Le cas des ethnies de la province de Bandundu*, Paris, L'Harmattan, 2007.

MBEMBE Achille, *Afriques indociles. Christianisme, pouvoir et Etat en société postcoloniale*, Paris, Karthala, 1988.

MBEMBE Achille, *Critique de la raison nègre*, Paris, La découverte, 2013.

MBEMBE Achille, *Sortir de la grande nuit: Essai sur l'Afrique colonisée*, Paris, Éditions le découverte, 2010,2013.

MBOG BATASSI Pierre-Éric, « Les moyennes sexuellement transmissibles frappent le Gabon », in *Afrik.com* du 5 Janvier 2008 consulté le 15 juin 2013.

MENI Malikwisha, « L'importance du secteur informel en RDC », in Bulletin de l'ANSD (Académie Nationale des Sciences du Développement, Volume I, Kinshasa, Décembre-Janvier 2000-2001.

MOROKVASIC Mirjana, « Le genre est au cœur des migrations » in FALQUET Jules et alii, *Le sexe de la mondialisation. Genre, classe, race et nouvelle division du travail*, Paris, Presses de la Fondation nationale des Sciences politiques, 2010.

MULUMA MUNANGA Albert, *Sociologie générale et africaine. Les sciences sociales et les mutations des sociétés africaines*, Préface de Clément Mwabila MALELA, Paris, L'Harmattan, 2008.

NDAYWEL-E-NZIEM Isidore, *Histoire du Zaïre. De l'héritage ancien à l'âge contemporain*, Louvain-la-Neuve, Duculot, 1997.

NKAY MALU Flavien, *La mission chrétienne à l'épreuve de la tradition ancestrale (Congo belge, 1891-1933)*, Paris, Karthala, 2007.

NSAKA KABUNDA Anne-Marie, « Espace public, espace masculin ? Politique et genre en République Démocratique du Congo » in CODESRIA 12e Assemblée générale tenue à Yaoundé du 7-11 décembre 2008.

PFEFFERKORN Roland, *Genre et rapports sociaux de sexe*, Lausanne, Éditions Page deux, 2012.

PFEFFERKORN Roland, *Inégalités et rapports sociaux. Rapports de classes, rapports de sexes,* Paris, La Dispute, 2007.

QUENUM Alphonse, *Les églises chrétiennes et la traite atlantique du XVe au XIXe siècles,* Paris, Les Éditions Karthala, 2008.

RADCLIFFE Timothy, o.p. « Quelle forme pour l'Église de demain ? », *La Documentation Catholique*, N°2432, du 18/10/2009.

REDIKER Marcus, *A bord du négrier. Une histoire atlantique de la traite,* Paris, Éditions du Seuil, 2013.

ROLLINDE Marguerite, « espace domestique, espace politique, espace économique : le genre franchit les frontières » in *Genre et changement social en Afrique,* Paris, Éditions des archives contemporaines.

SANTEDI Léonard, *Les défis de l'évangélisation dans l'Afrique contemporaine*, Paris, Karthala, 2005.

SCHLEGEL Jean-Louis, « Les religions avec, après ou contre les Lumières ? », *ESPRIT* n°357, Août-Septembre 2009.

SCHURE Edouard, *Les grands initiés*, Saint-Amand, Librairie académique Perrin, 1960.

SOME Roger, Préface à *Héritages silencieux*, Catalogue de l'exposition organisée par les étudiants du Master Muséologie de l'Université de Strasbourg, Metz, Éditions des Paraiges, 2014.

SOUDAN François et alii, « clandestins, voyage au bout de la honte » in *Jeune Afrique l'Intelligent,* 16 Octobre2005.

Stéphane de Tapia, *Système migratoire euro-méditerranéen. Effets des transferts financiers dans le pays d'origine,* Strasbourg, édition du conseil de l'Europe.

SOW Fatou, « Idéologies néolibérales et droits des femmes en Afrique » in FALQUET Jules et alii, *Le sexe de la mondialisation. Genre, classe, race et nouvelle division du travail*, Paris, Presses de la Fondation nationale des Sciences politiques, 2010.

THOMAS Louis Vincent, *Cinq essais sur la mort africaine*, Dakar, 1968.

THOMAS Louis Vincent, *Anthropologie de la mort*, Paris, Payot, 1976.

THOMAS Louis-Vincent, *La terre africaine et ses religions. Traditions et changements,* paris, l'Harmattan, 1980.

TOURAINE Alain, *Pourrons-nous vivre ensemble ? Égaux et différents*, Paris, Fayard, 1997.

VAN REYBROUCK David, *Congo. Une histoire*, Arles, Actes Sud, 2012.

VAN WING, *Études Bakongo II. Religion et magie. Mémoires*, Institut Royal Belge.

VERBEEK Léon, *Contes de l'inceste, de la parenté et de l'alliance chez les Bemba (RDC)*, Paris, Éditions Karthala, 2006.

ZAHAN Dominique, *Le feu en Afrique, culture et cosmologie,* Paris, l'Harmattan, 1995.

Contents

SMA Publications

in many leading bookstores like

iBooks.

Scribd.

SMA Sankofa series
Original unedited writings of our missionaries

Vol. 1.
Les circulaires des Préfets apostoliques de Côte d'Ivoire (1895-1911)

Vol. 2.
Mouren, Joseph, The catholic Missions in Northern Nigeria, Foundation and First Years (1906 – 1910)

Vol. 3.
Mouren, Joseph, Journal de la mission Bénoué-Tchad (1906-1909)

Available on all Amazon websites as paperback and ebook.

Biographies of our early missionaries (in French)
by Fr. Gilles Babinet

- *Melchior de Marion Brésillac (1813-1859),*
  Fondateur de la Société des Missions Africaines

- *Augustin Planque (1826-1907),*
  co-fondateur de la Société des Missions Africaines

- *Mgr Jean-Baptiste Chausse (1846-1894),*
  un missionnaire intrépide au pays yoruba

- *Mgr Louis Dartois (1861-1905),*
  premier Vicaire apostolique du Dahomey

- *Mgr François Faroud (1885-1963),*
  un pionnier au Sahel

- *Émile Barril (1874-1961),*
  Fondateur des Oblates Catéchistes Petites Servantes des Pauvres

www.ingramcontent.com/pod-product-compliance
Lightning Source LLC
Chambersburg PA
CBHW071351280526
45787CB00001B/282